THE
POPULAR SCIENCE

FACT BOOK
FOR INQUIRING MINDS

THE

100

GREATEST
UNSOLVED
MYSTERIES

THE
POPULAR SCIENCE
FACT BOOK
FOR INQUIRING MINDS
★ ★ ★

THE
100
GREATEST
UNSOLVED
MYSTERIES

Edited by
Susan Elkin

Cavendish
Square

New York

This edition published in 2018 by Cavendish Square Publishing, LLC
243 5th Avenue, Suite 136, New York, NY 10016

First Edition

Website: cavendishsq.com

This publication represents the opinions and views of the author based on his or her personal experience, knowledge, and research. The information in this book serves as a general guide only. The author and publisher have used their best efforts in preparing this book and disclaim liability rising directly or indirectly from the use and application of this book.

All websites were available and accurate when this book was sent to press.

Cataloging-in-Publication Data

Names: Elkin, Susan/ editor.
Title: The 100 greatest unsolved mysteries / Susan Elkin.
Description: New York : Cavendish Square, 2018. | Series: The popular science fact book for inquiring minds|
Includes bibliographical references and index.
Identifiers: ISBN 9781502632883 (library bound)
Subjects: LCSH: Science—Miscellanea—Juvenile literature.
Classification: LCC Q163.E455 2018 | DDC 500—dc23

Editorial Director: David McNamara
Editor: Michael Sciandra
Associate Art Director: Amy Greenan
Production Coordinator: Karol Szymczuk

PHOTO CREDITS

Images from: Andreas Trepte; Associated Press; Azcolvin429; Benjamin P. Horton; Caltech, NASA; Charlie Watson (USAID/Rainforest Alliance Forestry Enterprises); CIA; Damien Jemison/LLNL; DARPA; Dr. Mridula Srinivasan, NOAA/NMFS/OST/AMD; Dreamstime; ESO/A. Roquette; FermiBubble-NASA's Goddard Space Flight Center; Frank DeLeo, National Institute of Allergy and Infectious Diseases (NIAID); Frettie; Greg Sanders/USFWS H. G. Wells, Julian Huxley, G. P. Wells; Istock; J. Hester and P. Scowen (ASU), NASA; Library of Congress; Mandy Lindeberg, NOAA/NMFS/AKFSC; NASA; NASA/SkyWorks Digital; NASA_DOE_Fermi LAT Collaboration; X-ray, NASA_CXC_SAO; Infrared, NASA_JPL-Caltech; Optical, MPIA, Calar Alto, O. Krause et al. and DSS; NASA_JPL-Caltech_STScI_CXC_SAO' NASA_JPL-Caltech.jpg; NASAAmes-JPL-Caltech; NASA-CXC-M.Weiss NASA-Jim Yunge; NASA-JPL-Caltech-STScI; NASA-JPL-Caltech-UCLA; NASA-Pat Rawling; NASA, ESA, J. Hester, A. Lollcrabmosaic; NASA, ESA, M. J. Jee and H. Ford et al. (Johns Hopkins Univ.); NASA; ESA; G. Illingworth, D. Magee, and P. Oesch, University of California, Santa Cruz; R. Bouwens, Leiden University; and the HUDF09 Team; NASA/ESA/JHU/R.Sankrit & W.Blair; NASA/JPL-Caltech; NASA/JPL; NASA/Pat Rawlings, SAIC; NASA/Peter Reid, The University of Edinburgh; National Institute of Allergy and Infectious Diseases (NIAID/ NOAA) Pavel Riha; Shutterstock; Steffen Richter, Harvard University; Thinkstock; Thomas Schultz; U.S. Fish and Wildlife Service

22MEDIAWORKS (www.22mediaworks.com)
President Lary Rosenblatt
Designer Fabia Wargin Design
Editor Susan Elkin
Writers Charles Piddock, Susan Taylor, Susan Elkin,
Bonnie McCarthy
Copy-editor Laurie Lieb
Photo Researcher David Paul

Many thanks to Amy Bauman and Kevin Broccoli for editorial support.

Printed in the United States of America

Contents

PHYSICAL MATTER AND FORCES

10 Is Light a Wave or a Particle?
12 What Makes a Boomerang Come Back?
14 Is the Mpemba Effect Real?
15 What Is the Hottest
   Temperature Possible?
16 Is Cold Fusion Possible?
18 Do Atoms Last Forever?
19 Can We Travel Through Time?
20 Will We Ever Be Able to Harness
   Nuclear Fusion?
22 Does Spontaneous Human Combustion
   Ever Happen—and How?

SPACE

26 What Are Fermi Bubbles?
29 Why Do Pulsars Pulse?
30 Does Alien Life Exist?
31 Why Don't Moons Have Moons?
33 What Is the Moon Illusion?
34 What's at the Bottom of a Black Hole?
36 What Does Space Smell Like?
38 How Long Would It Take to
   Walk a Light-Year?
39 What Causes Jupiter's Red Storm?
40 Are There Habitable Planets Beyond
   Our Solar System?
42 What Is Dark Energy?
44 How Will the Universe End?
46 What Is the Shape of the Universe?
48 Can We Deflect Asteroids?
49 Why Is the Milky Way a Spiral?
51 Will We Find Other Universes?

52 Could We Live on Mars?
55 What Is Dark Matter Made Of?
56 What Causes Gamma Ray Bursts?
59 Is a Space Elevator Possible?
60 How Does Gravity Work?
62 How Do Stars Explode?
65 What Causes the Aurora Borealis?
66 Is a Holodeck Possible?
67 How Did Saturn Get Its Rings?
68 Could a Supernova Wipe Out
   Life on Earth?

HUMAN BODY

72 Why Do We Blush?
73 What Is the Evolutionary
   Purpose of Tickling?
74 Why Do We Yawn?
75 Why Are Peanut Allergies on the Rise?
76 What Is a Memory?
78 Why Do We Dream?
81 Why Do We Laugh?
82 Do Cells Make Noise?
84 How Does the Brain Work?
86 What Is Emotion?
87 Is It True That You Use Only
   10 Percent of Your Brain?
88 What Causes Déjà Vu?
90 Is the Y Chromosome Doomed?
91 Do Men and Women Have
   Different Brains?
92 Why Do We Sleep?
94 Why Do We Hiccup?
95 Why Aren't (Most) Humans Furry?

96   What Is the Science Behind Love?

98   Why Does Sunlight Make Some
     People Sneeze?

99   What Is Consciousness?

100 Can the Food You Eat Affect Your
     Descendants' Genes?

101 Are Telomeres the Key to Immortality?

103 Why Do We Have an Appendix?

104 Why Do We Have Fingerprints?

105 What Happens When You Die?

106 Is There an Alternative to DNA?

108 Why Do We Age?

109 When Will We Evolve Out of
     Our Useless Appendages?

110 How Much of the Human Body
     Is Replaceable?

111 Why Do Amputees Sense a
     "Phantom Limb"?

112 Can You Upload Your Brain
     to a Computer?

115 What Is Intelligence?

EARTH

118 What Causes Volcanic Lightning?

119 Just How Old Is Dirt?

120 How Do Plate Tectonics Work?

122 How Big Would a Meteorite Have to Be
     to Wipe Out All Human Life?

123 Are We Really Drinking Dinosaur Pee?

124 How Do Fire Tornadoes Form?

127 When Is the Next Ice Age Due?

128 Are Earthquake Lights Real or Illusory?

129 What Is Ball Lightning?

130 Why Can't We Predict Earthquakes?

131 Where Did Earth's Water Come From?

132 Why Do Earth's Magnetic Poles Flip?

133 How Do Icicles Form Under Water?

OTHER LIFE-FORMS

136 How Did Life Arise on Earth?

137 How Do Animals Sense
     Magnetic Fields?

138 How Do Animals Migrate?

139 Why Do Cats Purr?

140 Why Do Ducks Have Orange Feet?

141 Will Disease Drive Us All to Extinction?

142 What Do Whales Sing About?

144 Can We Clone Extinct Animals?

145 Could Cockroaches Survive
     a Nuclear Holocaust?

146 What Caused the Extinction
     of the Megafauna?

148 Why Are Bees Disappearing?

151 Why Do Geese Fly in a V Formation?

HUMAN TRIUMPHS AND TROUBLES

154 What Was the Purpose of Stonehenge?

156 How Were the Easter Island
     Statues Built?

159 What Happened to the Neanderthals?

160 Is the Doomsday Argument for Real?

162 Why Can't the Voynich Manuscript
     Be Deciphered?

164 Is the Antikythera Mechanism the
     World's First Analog Computer?

165 What Caused the Decline of the
     Mayan Civilization?

166 How Were the Pyramids Built?

168 **Glossary**

172 **Further Information**

173 **Index**

Physical Matter and Forces

CHAPTER 1

Is Light a Wave or a Particle?

For centuries, scientists debated the nature of light. Some claimed that light was a wave, behaving like a ripple in a pool. The opposing view was that light was a particle, like the droplets of water that flow from a kitchen faucet. Just when a prevailing view gained momentum, evidence for the other caused confusion. Finally, in the early 20th century, Albert Einstein called a tie: Light is both wave and particle.

Those who believed in the particle theory of light followed Sir Isaac Newton. He described light as a series of particles, using a prism to prove his theory. To Newton, the clarity and sharpness of the prism shadows meant that light traveled as a shower of particles, each following a straight line until disturbed.

Those who opposed Newton's theory followed scientist Christiaan Huygens, who cited light's diffraction and interference as proof that it is a wave. Diffraction, the bending of light as it passes around an object, and interference, when waves combine to form greater or lesser amplitude, occur in other mediums with wave-like properties, such as sound and water. Astronomers studying moving galaxies proved that light follows the Doppler Effect, the name for the change in sound as waves from the source move closer or farther away from you, elongating as they move away and shortening as they come closer. Visible light, as seen in the colors of the rainbow, exhibits similar properties, with longer wavelengths appearing as a red shift and shorter wavelengths as a blue shift. Until the turn of the century, this overwhelming evidence convinced most scientists that light was a wave, until Albert Einstein settled the score.

One thorn in the argument for light-as-a-wave purists is a phenomenon called the photoelectric effect. When light shines on a metal surface, electrons fly out. But

higher intensity of light does not cause more electrons to be released, as you would expect with the wave theory. Albert Einstein studied this effect and came up with a compelling theory that stated light was both wave and particle. Light flows toward a metal surface as a wave of particles, and electrons are released from the metal as an interaction with a single photon, or particle of light, rather than the wave as a whole. The energy from that photon transfers to a single electron, knocking it free from the metal. Einstein's declaration of wave-particle duality earned him the Nobel Prize in physics in 1921.

Since Einstein's discovery, physicists have embraced this theory. Einstein declared: "We have two contradictory pictures of reality; separately neither of them fully explains the phenomena of light, but together they do." Understanding light as a wave led to the development of important technology, such as lasers. The discovery of photons made possible the electron microscope.

And thanks to Albert Einstein, we can stop the centuries-old debate and declare everyone a winner.

What Makes a Boomerang Come Back?

Anthropologists theorize that the first boomerangs were heavy projectile objects thrown by hunters to bludgeon a target with speed and accuracy. They were most likely made out of flattened sticks or animal tusks, and they weren't intended to return to their thrower—that is, until someone unknowingly carved the weapon into just the right shape needed for it to spin. A happy accident, huh?

Proper wing design produces the lift needed for a boomerang's flight, says John "Ernie" Esser, a boomerang hobbyist who works as a postdoctoral researcher at the University of California at Irvine's Math Department. "The wings of a boomerang are designed to generate lift as they spin through the air," Esser says. "This is due to the wings' airfoil shape, their angle of attack, and the possible addition of beveling on the underside of the wings."

But a phenomenon known as gyroscopic precession is the key to making a returning boomerang come back to its thrower. "When the boomerang spins, one wing is actually moving through the air faster than the other [relative to the air] as the boomerang is moving forward as a whole," explains Darren Tan, a PhD student in physics at Oxford University. "As the top wing is spinning forward, the lift force on that wing is greater and results in unbalanced forces that gradually turn the boomerang." The difference in lift force between the two sides of the boomerang produces a consistent torque that makes the boomerang turn. It soars through the air and gradually loops back around in a circle.

THE BOOMERANG IS ONE OF HUMANITY'S OLDEST HEAVIER-THAN-AIR FLYING INVENTIONS. KING TUTANKHAMEN, WHO LIVED DURING THE FOURTEENTH CENTURY BCE, OWNED AN EXTENSIVE COLLECTION, AND ABORIGINAL AUSTRALIANS USED BOOMERANGS IN HUNTING AND WARFARE AT LEAST AS FAR BACK AS 10,000 YEARS AGO. THE WORLD'S OLDEST BOOMERANG, DISCOVERED IN POLAND'S CARPATHIAN MOUNTAINS, IS ESTIMATED TO BE MORE THAN 20,000 YEARS OLD.

To really make a boomerang soar, hold it vertically and give it a good spin—and be careful where you aim!

Is the Mpemba Effect Real?

For more than 2,000 years, scientists have observed the unique phenomenon that, in some conditions, hot water freezes faster than cold water. In the fourth century BCE, Greek scientist Aristotle noted, "The fact that the water has previously been warmed contributes to its freezing quickly: for so it cools sooner."

Seventeenth-century English scientist Francis Bacon noted, "slightly tepid water freezes more easily than that which is utterly cold." Several years later, French mathematician René Descartes echoed his predecessors' observations, writing, "One can see by experience that water that has been kept on a fire for a long time freezes faster than other."

Given the centuries-old knowledge that hot water does indeed freeze faster than cold in certain circumstances, it should have come as no surprise when Tanzanian schoolboy Erasto Mpemba claimed in his science class in 1963 that ice cream would freeze faster if it was heated first before being put into a freezer. "You were confused," said his teacher; "that cannot happen." Mpemba's assertion also amused his classmates—but their laughter quickly turned to a murmur of assent when a school supervisor ran the experiment and proved the young man correct.

Scientists have offered many explanations to account for the unexpected phenomenon, but to date none has been accepted by the wider scientific community. Here are a few suggestions:

EVAPORATION As the warmer water cools to the temperature of the cooler water, it may lose large amounts of water to evaporation. The reduced mass would more easily allow for the water to cool and freeze.

DISSOLVED GASES Hot water can hold less dissolved gas than cold water. This may somehow change the properties of the water, making it easier to develop convection currents, and therefore easier to freeze.

FROST Frost conducts heat poorly. If the containers of hot water are sitting on layers of frost, the water will cause the frost to melt. This would establish better thermal contact with the cold refrigerator shelf or floor.

To date, experiments have not adequately illustrated which, if any, of the proposed processes is the most important one. "It seems likely that there is no one mechanism that explains the Mpemba effect for all circumstances," explained Monwhea Jeng of the Department of Physics at the University of California, in 1998.

What Is the Hottest Temperature Possible?

It's easy to understand the theoretical minimum temperature: absolute zero. The absolute maximum, on the other hand, is squirrely. "We just don't know whether we can take energy all the way up to infinity," says Stephon Alexander, a physicist at Dartmouth University. "But it's theoretically plausible."

The most straightforward candidate for an upper limit is the Planck temperature, or 142 nonillion (1.42×10^{32}) kelvins (K), the highest temperature allowable under the Standard Model of particle physics. But temperature comes about only when particles interact and achieve thermal equilibrium, Alexander explains. "To have a notion of temperature, you need to have a notion of interaction."

Many cosmologists believe the hottest actual temperature in the history of the universe was several orders of magnitude cooler than the Planck temperature. In the first moments after the Big Bang, expansion occurred so rapidly that no particles could interact; the universe was essentially temperatureless. In the tiny slivers of a second that followed, Alexander says, ripples of space-time may have begun to vibrate with matter and forced that matter into thermal equilibrium. This would have caused a quick reheating of the universe to something like 10^{27} K. It has been continually expanding and cooling ever since.

Is Cold Fusion Possible?

Italian inventor Andrea Rossi really wants us to believe in cold fusion. He claims that his Energy Catalyzer, or E-Cat, a liter-sized device he designed, can output three times as much energy as it draws via low-energy nuclear reactions, or LENRs. As hydrogen passes over an electrified nickel-based catalyst, hydrogen nuclei supposedly fuse to the nickel, transmuting the metal into copper and releasing heat in the process. If we could harness that heat, the process could furnish cheap electricity while simultaneously banishing the production of greenhouse gases—all without creating any harmful waste.

There's only one problem: Modern evidence suggests that cold fusion is almost certainly a myth. Backers aside, Rossi has yet to perform a truly independent test of his E-Cat; in most tests by third parties, Rossi handled the materials or was involved in some way. Critics argue that Rossi's device doesn't produce nearly as much energy as he claims and that his suggestion of building factories for large-scale production of electricity is baseless. They also note that his backers refuse to publicly reveal themselves and that the physics behind the project are at best unclear.

Worst of all, every purportedly successful attempt at cold fusion up until now has been the result of experimental error or downright fraud. Martin Fleischmann and Stanley Pons, chemistry professors at the University of Utah, claimed they discovered cold fusion in 1989. No one has been able to replicate their results since and their ideas were discredited. Rusi Taleyarkhan, a Purdue University professor who claimed to have produced a "bubble fusion" reaction, was found guilty of "research misconduct." Besides, most physicists say that the findings just don't make sense: The energy required to bond hydrogen is simply too high for a catalyst to achieve at earthly temperatures.

Except in one case: Muon-catalyzed fusion is the only instance in which a catalyst is known to enable nuclear fusion. Muons are subatomic particles that occur on Earth principally as a result of cosmic rays slamming into the atmosphere. When muons replace the hydrogen atom's electrons, they can draw those hydrogen atoms close enough to fuse together. Unfortunately, muons require substantial energy to produce, and they don't last long enough for the chain reaction to produce more energy than goes into the reaction. Until physicists overcome these barriers, cold fusion will remain elusive.

Do Atoms Last Forever?

Despite what you may have heard, diamonds are not forever. Given enough time, your sparkling rock will degrade into common graphite. The carbon atoms that constitute that diamond, however, *are* forever, or close enough. Stable isotopes of carbon are thought to enjoy lifetimes that extend far longer than the estimated age of the universe.

But not every atom of carbon lives forever. Radioisotopes are forms of chemical elements with unstable nuclei and emit radiation during their decaying process to a stable state. Carbon-14, a radioisotope, is unstable, with a half-life less than 6,000 years; after 5,730 years, there is a 50 percent chance that a carbon-14 atom will lose an electron and become nitrogen-14 (which is itself stable and the most common form of nitrogen on Earth). Carbon-14 is the key element in carbon dating. Since radioactive carbon is only absorbed through respiration by living creatures, the date of their death can be determined by measuring the remaining carbon-14 in the specimen.

In addition to carbon-14, there are scores of other naturally occurring radioisotopes and more than a thousand manmade. Each of these radioisotopes tends to decay into another isotope: some in a matter of days, others in hundreds of millions of years. In this sense, these atoms do in fact die. In another way, however, they are simply reborn as different isotopes.

There is one mechanism by which even stable atoms might "die." Some exotic models of physics hypothesize that protons (which along with electrons and neutrons constitute atoms) can decay into lighter subatomic particles. Even if protons do decay, they are nevertheless incomprehensibly durable. Experiments put the lower bound of a proton's half-life at 10^{33} to 10^{34} years, or 23 orders of magnitude longer than the current age of the universe. In conclusion, atoms *are* forever on just about any relevant timescale.

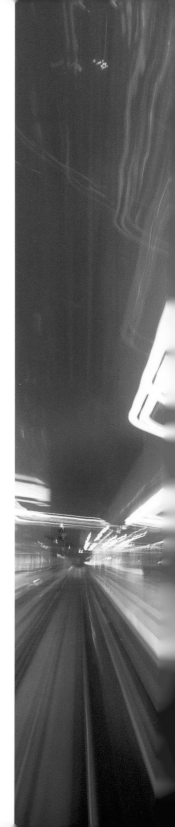

Can We Travel Through Time?

The mystery of time travel as it is portrayed in science fiction is not as simple as building a time machine. In fact, these fictional ideas require overturning Albert Einstein's special theory of relativity and somehow traveling close to the speed of light.

Physicists continue to ponder the possibilities of faster-than-light travel (FLT) and what it means for space exploration and our universe. The first example of faster-than-light speeds in popular culture occurred in the television series *Star Trek*, when "warp drive" sent spaceships traveling billions of light-years away in a matter of seconds. If this were possible, those space travelers might return to their original location and find that time had progressed at its usual speed, meaning 50 years may have passed during the short time the ship was absent, simulating time travel.

While most people view time as a constant, Einstein proved that time is relative to how fast an object moves according to its surroundings. Einstein pointed out that time is not a consistent flowing entity, but linked with space, and so the faster one travels through space, the more the perception of time changes, a phenomenon called time dilation. If an astronaut can somehow travel close to the speed of light, he will experience time differently than his friends left behind on Earth traveling at the usual speed. Time will pass much slower for the astronaut, and when he returns to Earth, his friends will have aged faster. However, the laws of physics state

that the speed of light is constant, represented by c in Einstein's famous equation $E = mc^2$. The speed of light in a vacuum is 186,282 miles per second (299,792 kms), and while some physicists have identified processes like quantum entanglement that travel faster than light, they do not carry mass or information. For a particle with mass, reaching the speed of light would require infinite acceleration and therefore infinite energy—an unrealistic accomplishment.

In 2011, physicists at the CERN institute in Switzerland thought they were close to a FLT discovery. A new subatomic particle called the neutrino, which carried a very small mass, appeared to travel faster than the speed of light. Their experiment launched particles from Switzerland to Italy, and the neutrinos arrived in Italy in record time, intriguing the world with thoughts of time travel and visits to distant galaxies. Unfortunately for CERN, the experiment was flawed. One cable was not properly connected, resulting in incorrect measurements.

According to Einstein's theory, objects with mass cannot exceed the speed of light because they would require an infinite amount of energy—be they spaceships or neutrinos. Even in all theoretical scenarios in which we travel faster than light, we can never travel backward in time, only forward. However, many scientists believe that traveling into the future is still a possibility that just needs more study. Wormholes, a theoretical passage through space-time that connects distant points in the universe, are attractive starting points for these theories. But however enticing the possibilities, it seems that success is still light-years away.

Will We Ever Be Able to Harness Nuclear Fusion?

The year is 2050. The carbon crisis is a thing of the past. A new source of power delivers cheap, plentiful electricity to large, contained cities populated by millions of people. Fusion power has birthed a utopia on Earth by neutralizing the most imminent threat to human survival, the finite supply of fossil fuel, while eliminating a persistent source of conflict. All is well—until a robotic alien from outer space destroys your fusion plant along with the rest of your city.

The scenario just described is familiar to anyone who grew up playing the popular 1990s simulation game SimCity 2000. As far as fusion power is concerned, the predictions of Maxis (the company that designed SimCity) from two decades ago seem prescient: Steve Cowley, a plasma physicist and the CEO of the United Kingdom's Atomic Energy Authority, expects the first viable demonstration reactors to be available sometime in the 2040s. That said, critics and proponents alike lament that nuclear fusion is "always 30 years away." What's changed? Recent breakthroughs indicate that the future of fusion is brighter than it has been in some time.

Physicists since the 1950s have been seeking to harness the power of the Sun. As it turns out, birthing a miniature star in a lab and keeping it under control is a difficult undertaking. The fusion reaction requires more energy than the reaction itself produces. It wasn't until October 2013 that any project broke even, when the National Ignition Facility (NIF) in California produced more energy than it consumed.

The success at the NIF, although exciting, is just another step on a long journey. To be commercially viable and to overcome basic inefficiencies in the conversion of raw energy into electricity, the reaction must continually produce *10 times* the amount of power that goes into it. Candidates for exceeding this threshold include the International Thermonuclear Experimental Reaction (known as ITER, pronounced "eater"), a project with the backing of seven countries that should come online by the end of the decade.

Recently, aerospace and technology giant Lockheed Martin's covert facility Skunk Works has announced a breakthrough in fusion technology that may yield results within the decade.

Secrecy still surrounds the research, but scientists hope that covert research facilities like Skunk Works will make "the impossible" possible.

Does Spontaneous Human Combustion Ever Happen—and How?

In 1980, Henry Thomas, a 73-year-old man living in Wales, was found burned to death in the easy chair of his living room—the trunk of his body nearly completely incinerated, but oddly, his feet unburned and the remains of his legs still clothed in socks and pants, practically untouched by the fire. Thomas's death was ruled "death by burning," although no cause of the apparent fire was noted.

In December 2010, the body of 76-year-old Michael Faherty was discovered burned beyond recognition in the living room of his home in Galway, Ireland. The damage caused by the fire was limited to Faherty's burned body, the ceiling above, and the floor beneath him. The coroner concluded Faherty's death "fit into the category of spontaneous human combustion."

Can human bodies spontaneously burst into flame without being ignited by an external source of heat? Most scientists would argue that humans cannot catch fire without an apparent cause. In fact, in the more than 200 cases of spontaneous human combustion (SHC) that have been reported worldwide, the true causes of death are far less fanciful than SHC.

In a study of 30 cases of alleged SHC, investigators Joe Nickell and John Fischer showed that candles, lamps, fireplaces, cigarettes, and other sources of heat were the likely reasons for ignition. Clothing, chair stuffing, and floor coverings usually provided additional fuel sources to sustain the fire.

One of the most commonly accepted explanations for alleged SHC is a phenomenon called the "wick effect." This theory suggests that an ignition source, such as a lit cigarette, will burn through the victim's clothing and into the skin. This releases body fat, which is absorbed into the clothing and burns like a candlewick. The fire will burn until the body's fat and the clothing are both consumed. Scientists believe such a "self-contained" fire is the reason victims' bodies are incinerated, yet their surroundings barely suffer damage.

"SHC is a non-explanation for bizarre burning deaths, no better than positing the attack of a fiery demon," says forensic analyst Nickell, "because there is not only no scientifically authenticated case of SHC but no credible mechanism by which it could happen."

Space

CHAPTER 2

What Are Fermi Bubbles?

In 2010, data gathered by the Fermi Gamma-Ray Space Telescope revealed a new discovery. Scientists were surprised to find two enormous, bubble-like clouds that extend 50,000 light-years across the center of our galaxy, the Milky Way.

**Fermi Bubbles extend
50,000 light-years,
roughly half of the
Milky Way's diameter.**

The two gamma-ray-emitting bubbles stretch across more than half of the visible sky and may be millions of years old. (Gamma rays are electromagnetic radiation at the highest-energy, or shortest-wavelength, end of the electromagnetic spectrum.) The origin of these previously unseen structures, however, remains a truly baffling mystery.

A research paper appearing in the *Astrophysical Journal* in 2014 described some features of the aptly dubbed "Fermi bubbles." First, the outlines of the structures are very sharp and well defined, and the bubbles glow evenly across their enormous surfaces. The most distant areas of the bubbles feature extremely high-energy gamma rays, yet there is no apparent cause for them that far from the galactic center. Lastly, the parts of the Fermi bubbles nearest the nucleus of the Milky Way contain both gamma rays and microwaves, but as the bubbles extend farther out, only the gamma rays are detectable.

Theorists have offered several explanations for the unusual structures. The two most predominant theories both suggest the bubbles were formed by a large, rapid energy release.

One possibility claims that enormous streams or jets of accelerated particles originating and blasting out of the supermassive black hole at the center of the Milky Way created the Fermi bubbles. Astronomers have observed such a phenomenon in other galaxies, and while it is unknown if the Milky Way black hole has an active jet today, it may have had one millions of years ago.

Another commonly held theory argues that the Fermi bubbles were created during star formations over a period of millions or even billions of years. The gas ejections created from bursts of star formations, similar to the ones that produced huge star clusters in the Milky Way, theoretically rode massive galactic winds out to far-off distances and are held there by powerful magnetic forces.

Scientists are eager to unravel the mystery of the Fermi bubbles' origin. "Whatever the energy source behind these huge bubbles may be," says David N. Spergel, a theoretical astrophysicist at Princeton University, "it is connected to the many deep questions in astrophysics."

Images taken with the Hubble Space Telescope show the Crab Nebula, the remains of a massive star explosion. In the center, the pulsar rotates approximately 30 times per second.

Why Do Pulsars Pulse?

Seven thousand years ago, a supermassive star in the constellation we now call Taurus collapsed in on itself and exploded into a supernova so bright that, when its light reached Earth in 1054 CE, it could be seen in broad daylight. What was left behind was the brilliant Crab Nebula, as well as the Crab Pulsar that illuminates it. This neutron star pulses out radiation across the entire electromagnetic spectrum at a rate of 30 times per second. But why does it pulse at all?

Only half a century ago, nobody knew that pulsars, short for "pulsating stars," existed. In 1967, when astronomers Jocelyn Bell Burnell and Antony Hewish first discovered a pulsating source of emissions all coming from the same point in the sky, among the first hypotheses was that these pulses were radio waves emitted by an alien civilization. Burnell and Hewish even went so far as to name the object LGM-1, short for "Little Green Men." Subsequent discoveries of new pulsars, including the Crab Pulsar, ruled out the alien emissions hypothesis.

Today, scientists know that pulsars are generated by rotating neutron stars. The stars rotate quickly due to the conservation of angular momentum: When a large rotating body collapses, the remaining matter spins at a much higher rate, akin to the effect spinning figure skaters experience when they hold their arms close against their body. Some of these neutron

stars have strong magnetic fields—in the case of pulsars, about 1 trillion times as strong as Earth's—and emit a beam of radiation that coincides with their magnetic poles. This radiation can be the result of the quickly spinning star's slowing momentum, the accretion of matter as it falls into the star, or the twisting of the star's magnetic field. This magnetic axis is not always the same as the axis of rotation. When they do not coincide, the beam of radiation wobbles about the rotational axis. The result of this wobbling is a beam of radiation that, when viewed from Earth, seems to be pulsating.

Since Burnell and Hewish first discovered pulsars, astronomers have identified nearly 2,000 more, emitting visible light, X-rays, and, in some cases, only gamma rays. And while we have a general idea of why pulsars pulse, astrophysicists believe that there is still much more to discover.

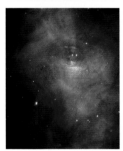

Stills from moving images of the Crab Nebula taken by the Hubble Space Telescope show movement within the pulsar. Scientists have estimated the exploded star is more than 10 light-years wide.

Does Alien Life Exist?

It's easy to proclaim that the existence of aliens is a crazy idea, until you consider these words from astrophysicist Stephen Hawking: "To my mathematical brain, the numbers alone make thinking about aliens perfectly rational. The real challenge is working out what aliens might actually be like."

Other scientists agree. But while the existence of alien life is mathematically probable, humans have not been able to prove that extraterrestrial life does exist. The quest to find that life has taken several forms. The Search for Extraterrestrial Intelligence (SETI) Institute, based in California, uses giant radio telescopes to try to detect radio signals sent by far-off, technically advanced life forms. NASA's Kepler Space Telescope has found planets within the Milky Way that could have the right conditions for life to develop. By one estimate, as many as 20 percent of the stars in the galaxy have such a suitable planet. A 2015 report highlighted one planet in particular, about 150 light-years away from Earth, that seemed like a possible candidate to support the development of alien life. It orbits a star called Epic 201367065, which is about half the size and mass of Earth's Sun.

While some people wonder about the complexity of possible alien life-forms, some scientists think it makes more sense to imagine "aliens" as simple microorganisms. Life on Earth started out as single cells, and life on other planets might still be at that stage of evolution. And as Hawking notes, Earth was lucky to avoid a cataclysmic collision with an asteroid or comet in the past 70 million years. Other planets could have had their early life-forms wiped out in such a cosmic crash.

NASA research done in the 1990s found what scientists thought were signs of ancient bacteria on a meteorite from Mars that reached Earth in 1984. Other scientists, though, dismissed the claim, and no one has proved the existence of microbes on Mars, now or in the past.

The possibility that the Red Planet once had water, however, was raised in 2014 after NASA scientists studied another meteorite from the planet that reached Earth. That same year, the NASA rovers, Curiosity and Opportunity, were able to capture high-resolution images of what are believed to be ancient riverbeds on the surface of Mars. The presence of water raises the possibility of biological activity as well. So does the discovery of large amounts of methane, which Curiosity also detected. The methane, however, could be the product of geochemical processes, rather than biological.

For now, scientists can feel confident in the odds that alien life does or did at some point exist, but without any idea of its form. As for the possibility of intelligent alien life ever visiting us on planet Earth, Hawking had this insight: The arrival of aliens could turn out to be much like Christopher Columbus's arrival in the Americas— and be followed by a steady stream of conquistadors and explorers from another universe. And we all know how that turned out for the people already living there.

Why Don't Moons Have Moons?

Astronomers can say with near certainty that there are no moons with moons in our solar system. But that doesn't mean it's physically impossible. After all, NASA has successfully put spacecraft into orbit around our moon.

Although astronomers have spotted some asteroids with moons, a parent planet's strong gravitational tug would make it hard for a moon to keep control of its own natural satellite, says Seth Shostak, a senior astronomer at the nonprofit Search for Extraterrestrial Intelligence (SETI) Institute. "You would need to have a wide space between the moon and planet," he says. Orbiting far from its parent planet, a relatively massive moon might be able to hold onto a moon of its own.

Conditions like these might exist in far-off solar systems, but while hundreds of exoplanets (planets outside of our solar system) have been detected, there's almost no chance we'll be able to spot exomoons, much less moons of exomoons, for decades to come. Most planet-hunting methods—such as spotting one as it passes a large star—lend themselves to detecting huge, Jupiter-like planets, or sometimes Earth-sized, rocky planets, but not their moons.

Even if astronomers spot a moon with a moon, it probably won't last long. "Tidal forces from the parent planet will tend, over time, to destabilize the orbit of the moon's moon, eventually pulling it out of orbit," says Webster Cash, a professor at the University of Colorado's Center for Astrophysics and Space Astronomy. "A moon's moon will tend to be a short-lived phenomenon."

What Is the Moon Illusion?

The Moon seems larger when it is near the horizon than when it is high in the sky, a phenomenon called the Moon illusion. Although recognized for centuries—the horizon Moon was important to early civilizations that functioned according to the Moon's cycle—this ancient phenomenon has only recently been explained.

Early astronomers believed the Moon at the horizon was physically closer to Earth than when it was high in the sky, and the closeness meant a larger Moon. However, Newton's description of the Moon's orbit showed the contrary to be true. The Moon is actually closest to the observer at its zenith, or when it is high in the sky, but the difference is so small that it is negligible anyhow. Others theorized that the Moon illusion was caused by refraction when light rays passed through more of Earth's atmosphere. Today, scientists guess that the illusion occurs not externally, but through a trick of our brains.

Optical illusions play a big role in the appearance of the Moon. When the Moon is placed as a backdrop against objects of known heights—such as trees, cars, or buildings—it appears larger than when it is isolated in the sky. In one experiment, researchers asked participants to view the horizon Moon through a cardboard tube, which caused background objects to disappear. They found the Moon seemed to shrink to a size similar to the zenith Moon.

The Ebbinghaus illusion describes this perceived effect. Two circles of identical size are placed near each other. One circle is surrounded by smaller circles, and the other circle is surrounded by larger circles. Although we know the original circles are identical, we perceive the circle surrounded by smaller circles as larger than the neighboring circle surrounded by larger circles. We also view the Moon as we do other objects, like clouds and birds, that recede into the skyline. We expect them to look smaller as they get farther away. In what is known as the Ponzo illusion, our brain tricks us into thinking the Moon is getting smaller as it rises in the sky, and in our minds only, farther away from Earth. But the Moon is still mostly the same distance away in its orbit. Nothing has changed in its size or its distance from our planet. To practice this, draw two identical parallel lines horizontally across a photo of a receding railroad track. The line closest will appear smaller than the line farther away, because as the tracks recede into the horizon, they become smaller, and your brain expects the line to do the same.

Still not convinced? Try taking a picture of the large Moon at the horizon. The camera doesn't suffer from the same visual cues that make the Moon appear as massive as in real life. This illusion is not unique to the Moon—the Sun and stars show the same properties. And while interesting to consider, the Moon illusion offers little insight into astronomy and the atmosphere. Instead, it proves an example of optical illusion.

What's at the Bottom of a Black Hole?

Black holes are already among the most mysterious objects in the universe, even before we begin to contemplate what might be at the "bottom" of one. The concept of a tiny star whose gravitational field is so strong that neither light nor matter can escape was so foreign to those who first theorized their existence that even Albert Einstein himself, whose math confirmed their possibility, dismissed the likelihood of their existence. As to the question of what's at the bottom, the answer—depending on the physicist— may be just about anything, or nothing, or even another universe.

At the outer edge of a black hole is the event horizon, the boundary where velocity required to escape its gravity exceeds the speed of light. Past this point, all energy and matter that enter the black hole will proceed infinitely toward the singularity, a point of infinite density that, according to Einstein's theory of general relativity, represents a bottomless pit of space-time. If the hole is truly infinite and nothing can escape past the event horizon, then the bottom of a black hole could theoretically hold an infinite amount of matter and energy.

However, while that interpretation may square with general relativity, the laws of thermodynamics maintain that a system cannot infinitely increase its mass while maintaining a similar temperature and level of disorder. Other theories that account for black hole thermodynamics suggest that anything falling toward the event horizon never really reaches the singularity, eventually evaporating back into space. According to astrophysicist Stephen Hawking, this is because black holes aren't truly black: They emit a minute amount of radiation, far less than the background radiation of space, but enough to eventually return the mass of the black hole back to the rest of the universe.

Other more exotic theories posit that at the bottom of a black hole lies an entire universe. How can this be? The combination of the insanely high temperatures, densities, and rotational velocity at the center of a black hole is so powerful that it could produce a massive expansion in space-time that might give rise to a new universe—a process not unlike that of the Big Bang that gave rise to our own universe. The logical extension of this theory implies that even our universe may lie at the bottom of a black hole.

The mystery has only deepened of late as prominent astrophysicists (including Hawking) change their minds on whether black holes even exist. According to Hawking and others, the laws of quantum mechanics may prevent a neutron star from collapsing beyond a small enough radius to fit within its event horizon. This would mean that no black hole is ever small enough for its escape velocity to exceed the speed of light, and thus there is no black hole.

What Does Space Smell Like?

The final frontier smells a lot like a NASCAR race—
a bouquet of hot metal, diesel fumes, and barbecue.
The source? Dying stars.

The by-products of all this combustion are smelly compounds called polycyclic aromatic hydrocarbons. These molecules "seem to be all over the universe," says Louis Allamandola, the founder and director of the Astrophysics and Astrochemistry Laboratory at NASA Ames Research Center. "And they float around forever," appearing in comets, meteors, and space dust. These hydrocarbons have even been short-listed as the basis of the earliest forms of life on Earth. Not surprisingly, polycyclic aromatic hydrocarbons can be found in coal, oil, and even food.

Though a pure, unadulterated whiff of outer space is impossible for humans (space is a vacuum, after all; we would die if we tried), we can get an indirect sense of the scent: When astronauts work outside the International Space Station, spaceborne compounds adhere to their suits and hitch a ride back into the station. Astronauts have reported smelling "burned" or "fried" steak after a space walk, and they aren't just dreaming of a home-cooked meal.

The smell of space is so memorable and distinct that, three years ago, NASA asked Steven Pearce of the fragrance maker Omega Ingredients to re-create the odor for use in its training simulations. "Recently we did the smell of the Moon," Pearce says. "Astronauts compared it to spent gunpowder."

Allamandola explains that our solar system is particularly pungent because it is rich in carbon and low in oxygen, and "just like a car, if you starve it of oxygen, you start to see black soot and get a foul smell." Oxygen-rich stars, however, have aromas reminiscent of a charcoal grill.

Once you leave our galaxy, the smells could get really, really interesting. In dark pockets of the universe, molecular clouds full of tiny dust particles may host a veritable smorgasbord of odors, from wafts of sweet sugar to the rotten-egg stench of sulfur.

How Long Would It Take to Walk a Light-Year?

If you had started just before the first dinosaurs appeared, you'd probably be finishing your hike just about now.

Here's how it breaks down. One light-year—the distance light travels in one year, used as the yardstick for interstellar distances—is about 5.9 trillion miles (9.5 trillion km). If you hoofed it at 20 minutes a mile, it would take 225 million years to complete your journey (not including stops for meals or the restroom). Even if you hitched a ride on NASA's Mach 9.8 X-43A hypersonic scramjet, it would take more than 90,000 years to cover the distance.

You'd need to bring a big backpack, too: Walking such a distance requires substantial supplies. The average adult burns about 80 calories per mile walked, so you'd need about six trillion granola bars to fuel your trip. You'd also produce a heap of worn-out shoes. The typical pair of sneakers will last you 500 miles (800 km), so you'd burn through some 11.8 billion pairs. And all that effort wouldn't get you anywhere, astronomically speaking: The closest star to the Sun, Proxima Centauri, is 4.22 light-years away.

JUPITER'S GREAT RED SPOT IS A HIGH-PRESSURE STORM THAT HAS BATTERED THE PLANET CONSISTENTLY FOR 400 YEARS. ITS SIZE IS SO GREAT THAT YOU CAN SEE IT WITH A BACKYARD TELESCOPE.

What Causes Jupiter's Red Storm?

At one time, the storm was at least 20,000 miles (32,000 km) in diameter and big enough to envelop three Earths. It is similar to a hurricane on Earth, rotating counterclockwise with a maximum wind speed of 268 miles per hour (430 kmh), almost twice as fast as the worst hurricanes on Earth. Historic observations date as far back as the 1600s. Since then, the spot has changed, fluctuating between a deep red and a pale salmon color. Laboratory experiments suggest that complex organic molecules, red phosphorus, and other sulfur compounds cause the vibrant color. But since the 1930s, the storm has shrunk to half its largest diameter. Even though it may be dwindling in size, the longevity and enormity of our solar system's biggest storm is full of mystery.

The reason for the persistence of the Great Red Spot is unknown, but presumably comes from the fact that it never moves over land, unlike hurricanes on Earth. Jupiter is composed of hydrogen and a small amount of helium and has no "land" in its form. Jupiter's internal heat source is a driving force, and the spot tends to absorb nearby weaker storms. However, based on computer models, the spot should have disappeared after several decades. Waves and turbulence in and around the storm sap it of energy. The powerful jet streams that surround the spot should slow its spinning. And even though the storm absorbs smaller ones, researchers say that doesn't happen enough to explain the storm's longevity. Some scientists think vertical flows in the storm are just as important

as the more-studied horizontal flows. When the storm loses energy, vertical flows move hot and cold gases in and out of the storm, restoring energy.

Understanding Jupiter's red storm could reveal more clues about the vortices in Earth's oceans and also the nurseries of stars and planets. Philip Marcus, a fluid dynamicist and planetary scientist at the University of California at Berkeley, explains the importance of understanding the Great Red Spot: "Vortices with physics very similar to the GRS are believed to contribute to star and planet formation processes, which would require them to last for several million years"— even as the Great Red Spot shrinks, it retains enormous significance for Earth and the very beginnings of the solar system.

Are There Habitable Planets Beyond Our Solar System?

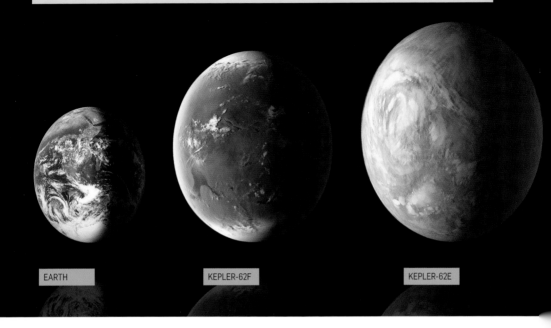

EARTH KEPLER-62F KEPLER-62E

Ever since people first tilted their gaze up toward the heavens, they have wondered about the possibility of other worlds like ours orbiting distant suns. Until very recently, such questions were left to the realm of speculation. Today, thanks to telescopes like the Kepler space observatory and increasingly advanced surveys from ground-based technology, we know that the galaxy is swarming with planets. But are any of them habitable? Do any of them resemble our own?

The question of habitability is a tricky one, and the odds of any individual planet possessing Earth-like properties are rather low. That said, the numbers are in our favor. Kepler recently confirmed the discovery of its 1,000th exoplanet. Some astronomers now estimate that there is one exoplanet for every star, on average. That means there are billions and billions of planets in our universe! Many of these planets, though, are nothing close to habitable. The first exoplanets that astronomers found orbited impossibly close to their suns, tidally locked, exposing one side to scorching heat and radiation and the other side to permanent night. In contrast, Earth orbits the Sun in the so-called Goldilocks Zone: not so close that all liquid water boils away, but not so far that it is perpetually frozen in ice.

RELATIVE SIZES OF HABITABLE ZONE PLANETS

Illustrated representations of exoplanets that have potential to support life as we know it. They are ranked here closest to farthest from Earth.

KEPLER-69C

KEPLER-22B

What's water got to do with the existence of other planets? The capacity to harbor liquid water is the key characteristic that astronomers look for in the search for habitable alien worlds, due to water's paramount importance to life on our own planet. But liquid water and a planet's average orbital distance are but two of several key factors. For instance, the class of star that serves as the sun is important: Habitability requires a sun that emits the right type of radiation and is likely to live long enough to allow life to evolve. A stable orbit is also important, ensuring that the planet's climate doesn't fluctuate wildly. The mass of the planet—massive enough so that it's capable of generating and holding onto an atmosphere, but not so massive that the atmosphere is oppressively dense—is also critical.

While astronomers have not yet confirmed the presence of habitable exoplanets, all signs currently point to the affirmative. Scientists reviewing data from the Kepler observatory recently discovered eight planets, roughly the size of Earth, in their respective sun's Goldilocks Zone. Other candidates exist, from as nearby as 40 light-years to thousands of light-years distant, some orbiting superclose to colder suns, and some much larger than Earth; so-called super-Earths range in size from two to 10 Earth masses. We seem to be on the verge of discovering a planet that might not only be capable of supporting life, but could hypothetically support life.

Whether these habitable planets already support life-forms and whether those life-forms are intelligent—well, that's a whole other mystery.

What Is Dark Energy?

In 1929, American astronomer Edwin Hubble studied a number of exploding stars, or supernova, and determined that the universe was expanding. The notion that distant galaxies were moving away from ours was a radical idea.

It seemed obvious to astronomers that gravity—the mutual attraction between all matter—would affect the expansion process. But how? Would the pull of gravity completely halt the expansion of the universe? Could the universe stop expanding and then reverse itself back toward us? Or would the universe eventually escape the gravitational effect and continue to expand? The universe may be expanding, reasoned the scientific community, but its expansion was surely slowed by the forceful effects of gravity.

Fast forward nearly 70 years to a time when two teams of astrophysicists—one led by Saul Perlmutter at the Lawrence Berkeley National Laboratory and the other by Brian Schmidt at Australian National University—began studying supernovas to calculate the assumed deceleration of expansion. To their astonishment, they discovered that supernovas as far as 7 billion light-years away were not brighter than expected but rather dimmer, meaning they were more distant than the teams had calculated them to be. The universe isn't slowing down, they concluded. It's speeding up.

The discovery turned the scientific world on its head: If gravity isn't the most dominant force in the universe, what is? In 1998, American theoretical cosmologist Michael S. Turner dubbed the mysterious new something "dark energy." Yet even with a name, we know little about dark energy.

Theorists have come up with several explanations for dark energy. The leading theory claims that dark energy is a property of space. Albert Einstein claimed it is possible for more space to come into existence and that "empty space" can have its own energy. "As more space comes into existence," reports NASA, "more of this energy-of-space would appear. As a result, this form of energy would cause the universe to expand faster and faster."

NASA reports that scientists have been able to theorize how much dark energy there is out there because we know how it affects the expansion of the universe. Roughly 69 percent of the universe is dark energy. Dark matter accounts for about 27 percent, leaving the rest—all normal matter, everywhere—adding up to less than 5 percent of the universe.

Another explanation posits that dark energy is a new type of energy field or energy fluid that fills space but affects the expansion of the universe differently than matter and normal energy. Scientists have labeled this energy "quintessence," but we still don't know what it interacts with or why it even exists.

In this illustration, dark energy, a force found throughout the universe and theorized to stimulate its expansion, is represented by the purple color. The green grid represents gravity.

For now, the mystery of dark energy continues to confound scientists. The NASA website concludes, "The thing that is needed to decide between dark energy possibilities—a property of space, a new dynamic fluid, or a new theory of gravity—is more data, better data."

How Will the Universe End?

An image of a small area of space in the constellation Fornax, created using Hubble Space Telescope data from 2003 and 2004. By collecting faint light over many hours of observation, the data revealed thousands of galaxies, both nearby and very distant, making it the deepest image of the universe ever taken at that time.

In 1929, Edwin Hubble discovered that the universe is not in fact static, but expanding. In the years following his discovery, cosmologists took up the implications of the discovery, asking how long the universe had been expanding, what forces caused the expansion, and whether it will ever cease.

Cosmologists are pretty confident about the first question: just shy of 14 billion years. A great deal of evidence supports the predominant answer to the second question: The universe rapidly emerged from a singularity in an event that cosmologists call the Big Bang. The third question is a bit more mysterious, and the answer relies on an obscure, confounding phenomenon known as dark energy. The density of dark energy in the universe determines its ultimate fate. In one scenario, the universe does not possess enough dark energy to forever counteract its own gravity and thus ends in a "Big Crunch." Under this scenario, the universe's gravity will overcome its expansion and the cosmos will collapse in on itself, resulting in a singularity that may precipitate another Big Bang. However, the evidence cosmologists have gathered over the last few decades leads us away from this scenario.

For the Big Crunch to occur, we'd see signs that gravity was winning out over dark energy, slowing its expansion. However, measurements of distant galaxies indicate that cosmic expansion is not slowing down—it's speeding up! Apparently, the density of dark energy in the vacuum of space is simply too high to permit a Big Crunch.

Some say the world will end in fire
Some say in ice.

— ROBERT FROST

This is the way the world ends
Not with a bang but a whimper.

— T.S. ELIOT

That leaves two possible fates for the cosmos: 1) a Big Freeze, in which the acceleration eventually halts but the universe keeps expanding, creating a system where heat becomes evenly distributed, allowing no room for usable energy to exist and thus, "heat death," or 2) a Big Rip, in which the expansion of the universe continues to accelerate forever. In the former scenario, the universe will progressively become darker and colder until the end of time. In the latter, all matter down to the most fundamental particles will be torn asunder.

All the recent data from the Planck space observatory and the Sloan Digital Sky Survey suggest there is just enough dark energy to continue the universe's expansion, but not enough to keep it accelerating forever. This conclusion points toward the Big Freeze, or "heat death" of the universe. The most up-to-date science leads us to the conclusion that our universe—and Robert Frost's—is more likely to end in ice than in fire. That, however, assumes that what we believe about dark energy is true. Considering that dark energy itself is a phenomenon cloaked deeply in mystery, such assumptions may yet prove untenable.

What Is the Shape of the Universe?

Most casual observers would assume that the cosmos is a space that expands into infinity, but the answer is not as simple as gazing into a starry sky and hazarding a measurement. Einstein's theory of general relativity, when paired with estimates of the relative amounts of matter and energy in the cosmos, allows for only one possible solution— the universe is infinite.

General relativity requires that the universe remain the same throughout (homogeneity) and appear the same in all directions (isotropy). Therefore, the shape of the universe is the result of the push and pull of gravity and dark energy. This may sound familiar. The same characteristics determine the universe's three possible fates: the Big Crunch, the Big Rip, and the Big Chill.

Just as a universe with an energy density less than its gravitational pull will eventually collapse in on itself (the Big Crunch scenario), the same gravity will overcome dark energy to mold the universe into a sphere. A spherical universe implies that there is a finite amount of space (just as there is a finite amount of surface on a sphere), that two lines appearing parallel will eventually converge (just as lines of longitude on Earth converge as they approach the poles from the equator), and that by traveling far enough we can return to our original position.

Conversely, a universe with an energy density greater than its gravitational pull will exhibit the opposite geometry, better resembling a saddle than a sphere. In such a universe, the

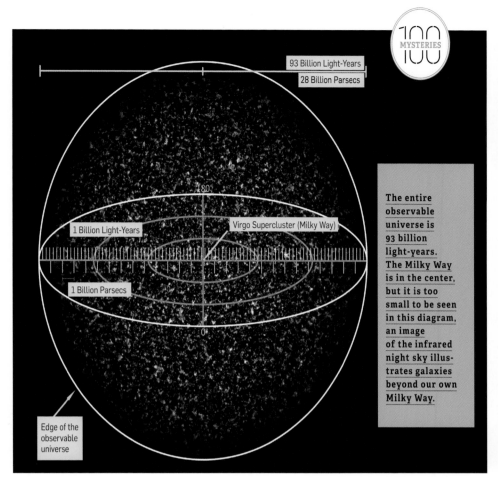

93 Billion Light-Years

28 Billion Parsecs

180°

1 Billion Light-Years

Virgo Supercluster (Milky Way)

1 Billion Parsecs

0°

Edge of the observable universe

The entire observable universe is 93 billion light-years. The Milky Way is in the center, but it is too small to be seen in this diagram, an image of the infrared night sky illustrates galaxies beyond our own Milky Way.

overwhelming force of dark energy pulls the universe into an inverted curve where initially parallel lines will gradually diverge. Much like the previous scenario, this universe is still finite.

However, just as cosmologists are fairly confident that the cosmos will not end its life in a Big Rip or Big Crunch, they are equally confident that the geometry of the universe is neither spherical nor saddle-shaped. When both gravity and dark energy reach a balance in their effect on the cosmos, the math implies that the universe will simply stretch out forever as an infinite flat plane. In this universe, two initially parallel lines remain parallel forever, and we will never be able to return to our starting point by traveling any distance in the same direction.

It is worth noting that confidence in this measurement depends on the correctness of Einstein's assumptions about homogeneity and isotropy as well as the accuracy of the current understanding of dark matter. These assumptions underlie the standard models of cosmology, but should they prove even marginally inaccurate, we could be living in a much different universe indeed.

Can We Deflect Asteroids?

Will an asteroid hurtling through space some day crash into Earth and cause massive damage? The odds are small, but they're real. Deflecting an incoming asteroid might seem like the stuff of science fiction, but scientists say it can be done—if the asteroid is detected in time. Given enough prior knowledge, former US astronaut Ed Lu says, governments could launch one or more spacecraft into the threatening asteroid and change its path enough so that it would miss Earth. These "kinetic impactors," Lu says, could even divert an asteroid the size of the one that brought down the dinosaurs.

Lu is one of the co-founders of the B612 Foundation, a non-profit organization that monitors asteroids and other Near Earth Objects (NEO) and studies how to protect Earth from them. Its goal is to fund the building and launch of a space telescope named Sentinel. The telescope, scheduled for launch in 2018, will map all the asteroids around Earth. Realizing the threat of an asteroid collision is real, in 2013 the United Nations called for the creation of the International Asteroid Warning Network. The goal is to bring together scientific organizations and nations with active space programs so they can share knowledge about the asteroid threat.

Why Is the Milky Way a Spiral?

The shape of our galaxy is nothing special. Among the other clusters of stars that can be easily observed from our corner of the universe, a few are blobby and egg-shaped, but more than two-thirds are so-called "disc galaxies" whose stars have settled into flat orbits, as if traveling along the surface of a giant vinyl record. Almost every disc galaxy looks at least a bit like ours, with stars that group together into spiral arms.

What causes the spirals? "A galaxy is constantly bombarded by satellite galaxies," says Chris Purcell of West Virginia University. When one galaxy passes by or through another, the resulting forces can send a shock wave throughout its structure, bunching stars together in spindly shapes that rotate around the center. "It's essentially a vibration that travels gravitationally throughout the disc," Purcell explains. As a galaxy ages, these perturbations tend to mount, and the disc goes from being thin, circular, and relatively homogeneous to thicker and more distorted. It's a natural process, says Purcell: "These galaxies are not only trying to turn themselves into spirals; they are constantly getting banged into by things that are turning them into spirals."

The Milky Way would seem to be somewhat early in the process, as evidenced by its slender figure. But things are changing: Several of the other, smaller galaxies are now (on a cosmological timescale) bumping up against us. One of these is the Sagittarius Dwarf. "It turns out that it's on the opposite side of the galaxy from us," Purcell says, "and so it's hitting the disc from underneath." Purcell's simulations suggest that these collisions could account for the spiral that we see today.

An even more extreme collision could be in our future. "We're on our first in-fall toward Andromeda," Purcell warns. "It's going to destroy both discs and turn the entire system into an elliptical blob." But let's not get ahead of ourselves: That crash is still more than a billion years off.

100 MYSTERIES

WRAPPED UP IN OUR OWN DAILY TRIALS, IT'S HARD TO IMAGINE LIFE OUTSIDE OF EARTH, LET ALONE IN AN ALTERNATIVE UNIVERSE. BUT ACCORDING TO SOME SCIENTISTS, THERE MAY BE AN INFINITE NUMBER OF ALTERNATIVE UNIVERSES, ALSO CALLED MULTIVERSES, AND FINDING THEM IS NOT ONLY POSSIBLE, BUT PROBABLE.

The Dark Sector Lab (DSL), shown above, located 0.75 of a mile (1.2 km) from the Geographic South Pole, houses the BICEP2 telescope (*left*) and the South Pole Telescope (*right*).

Will We Find Other Universes?

There are several theories of the multiverse. One comes from the "many worlds" interpretation of quantum physics by Hugh Everett. In 1955, over a bottle of sherry while a student at Princeton University, Everett considered the implications of quantum physics. At the elementary level (protons and electrons), each particle exists in a superposition of different locations, velocities, and orientations of its spin, but when measured by scientists there is a definitive result. Somehow our unique world emerges in a system that has a multitude of possibilities at the quantum, or nanoscopic, level. In this theory, every possible outcome in the universe exists simultaneously in other universes. For example, if you shoot a basketball and miss, there is a parallel reality in which your basketball slides right through the net. This alternative universe doesn't occupy a physical space, but is instead a co-existing, abstract reality. However, for many physicists, understanding and proving this alternative reality is too far afield.

Another type of multiverse is conceivable through a theory called inflation. In the first moments after the Big Bang, the universe expanded exponentially, traveling faster than the speed of light. Some theorists suggest that random quantum fluctuations in the early universe caused this inflation to stop in some regions but not in others. In places where inflation stopped, pocket universes formed, where atoms, stars, and even planets could assemble. Our universe may even be one of the myriad of pocket universes. Recently, this theory gained momentum as physicists behind the BICEP2 telescope in Antarctica found ripples in the space-time fabric of the cosmos called gravitational waves. The unique pattern in the sky reinforced the inflation theory.

But traveling to one of these alternate universes may be impossible. Each pocket universe would exist as a bubble, with its own laws of physics. The bubbles are connected, but in between them, eternal inflation is still stretching space-time faster than the speed of light. Even if we could somehow travel faster than light, the journey would be rough. As Anthony Aguirre, a physicist at the University of California at Santa Cruz, explains, "You also have to survive the inflation in between that would want to inflate every atom in your body. It's not very practical."

The BICEP2 telescope at twilight, which occurs only twice a year at the South Pole. The MAPO observatory (home of the Keck Array telescope) and the South Pole station can be seen in the background.

Could We Live on Mars?

What happens when the human population outpaces the resources of our planet? Many people wonder if moving humankind to another planet is possible. Scientists agree that of all the other planets in our solar system, Mars would be the most habitable, but that's not saying much. If the goal is to create a self-sustaining Martian world, life will be difficult and dangerous.

Mars has some similarities to Earth. Its axial tilt is about the same, so Mars experiences similar seasons; however, its orbital eccentricity is much larger, so the length of the seasons varies and a year lasts almost twice as long as on Earth. The length of a day is about the same. The desert terrain is similar to some regions on Earth. However, despite these similarities, Mars is a completely hostile environment. There is no breathable air and very little air pressure. Lower gravity presents problems for prolonged settlement. Temperatures vary widely: While they may climb as high as 70 degrees Fahrenheit (21 degrees Celsius), in some places they drop as low as minus 225 degrees (-142 degrees Celsius). The soil is toxic, and radiation from the Sun is deadly. All this may seem a little too out-of-this-world, but some scientists and a few entrepreneurs hope to make the dream of life on Mars a reality.

Technology will be a major player in a successful Mars settlement. Residents will require constant pressurized and heated environments. Luckily, the planet provides a few raw materials, such as soil, to make concrete. Mars is home to several large caves, which would screen settlers from radiation. Residents may be able to grow plants after removing

harsh chemicals from the toxic soil. Water on the fourth planet from the Sun is available, but the atmosphere is too thin for liquid water to exist for long. Instead, water is trapped just under the surface of the polar regions. Extracting water would be vital for drinking, growing food, and producing oxygen.

Space is opening up to the private sector, and a few companies are taking one small step toward life on Mars. Elon Musk, the founder of SpaceX, a space exploration and technology company, aims to build a colony of 80,000 people. SpaceX announced plans to put humans on Mars as early as 2026, 10 years ahead of NASA. But getting to Mars isn't as difficult as landing, surviving on the planet, or even returning to Earth. Musk told CNBC, "the thing that matters long term is to have a self-sustaining city on Mars, to make life multiplanetary," indicating that Mars could be a refuge in case we outgrow our current planet. Given Earth's dwindling resources, that could be sooner than we think.

The shadowy ring in this galaxy cluster, captured by the Hubble Space Telescope, is evidence of dark matter, a mysterious substance that pervades the universe.

What Is Dark Matter Made Of?

As far back as the 1930s, evidence for the existence of a "dark matter" in the universe began to emerge.

Swiss astronomer Fritz Zwicky measured the velocities of several galaxies in the Coma cluster, a group of more than 1,000 identified galaxies, and concluded that many of them were moving so fast that they should have escaped the gravitational pull of the other galaxies. Zwicky, and other astronomers noticing the same phenomenon, concluded "that something we have yet to detect is providing these galaxies with additional mass, which generates the extra gravity they need to stay intact. This "something" is invisible—hence the nickname "dark matter."

But exactly what is dark matter, and what is it made of?

NASA notes that we're "more certain what dark matter is not than we are what it is." Dark matter does not take the form of stars and planets we can see, yet it constitutes about 27 percent of all the matter in the universe. It is not made of baryonic matter, the protons, electrons, and neutrons that make up regular space matter such as stars, planets, rocks, and gas clouds. It does not absorb, emit, or reflect light—the very reason it is extremely difficult to see. In fact, we can only infer its existence based on its gravitational effects on the motions of galaxies and stars.

So what is dark matter made of? The most common view is that dark matter is composed of weakly interacting massive particles, or WIMPS. These particles interact weakly with baryonic matter via gravity. WIMPS have as

much as 100 times the mass of a proton, but their weak interactions with baryonic matter make them nearly impossible to see.

Other nonbaryonic candidates include neutralinos, hypothetical heavy particles; the smaller neutrinos, subatomic particles without charge; and photinos, a hypothetical subatomic particle. Some scientists believe that dark matter may be composed of bodies of baryonic matter that emit little light and drift through space unattached to any single solar system. Because they emit no light, these bodies, called massive compact halo objects, or MACHOs, would be difficult to detect.

A clearer understanding of the composition of dark matter could help scientists better understand the nature of our universe—especially, how galaxies hold together.

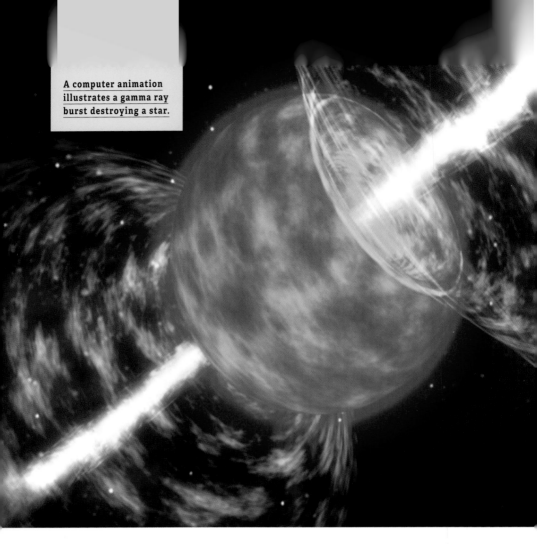

A computer animation illustrates a gamma ray burst destroying a star.

What Causes Gamma Ray Bursts?

Imagine a single blast of energy powerful enough to destroy the equivalent of a thousand Earths in a second. Explosions of that magnitude happen in the universe every day, thanks to gamma ray bursts. Scientists didn't know these extreme bursts of energy existed until the 1960s, when satellites designed to monitor nuclear weapons tests on Earth picked up the phenomenon.

Along the electromagnetic spectrum of energy—which includes radio waves, ultraviolet waves, and visible light—gamma rays are the most powerful. A gamma ray burst is a focused stream of energy that can last from just a few seconds to several minutes. Just one 10-second burst releases more energy than our Sun will produce over its 10-billion-year lifetime. Most bursts occur outside the Milky Way in galaxies with many massive stars.

Today scientists have two main theories to explain what might cause a gamma ray burst. One idea involves neutron stars. If two of these massively dense stars orbit each other and their orbits start to decay because of gravitational pull, they collide. That collision creates a black hole. Before some of the stars' matter tumbles into the black hole, it releases energy that some scientists think produces a gamma ray burst.

The second theory gives hypernovas credit for the bursts. The "death" of a star with a mass 10 times greater than the Sun's creates an explosion called a supernova. The death of an even more massive star creates a hypernova explosion. Hypernovas might cause some gamma ray bursts. Scientists also consider that both theories might be accurate: Neutron star collisions create short bursts, and hypernovas create longer ones. Or, another process the scientists haven't considered could explain all the bursts.

Knowing what causes gamma ray bursts may not be as important as understanding how they could affect Earth. In 2014, astronomers Tsvi Piran and Raul Jimenez calculated fairly high odds that a past gamma ray burst caused a mass extinction of life on Earth. Long-ago bursts might also explain why humans have not yet found life on other planets.

NEXT STOP:
11,740,608TH FLOOR.
HOUSEWARES! LINGERIE!
GEOSTATIONARY ORBIT!

Is a Space Elevator Possible?

New developments in nanotechnology have scientists hopeful that the idea of a space elevator should no longer be relegated to the imagination of futurists and sci-fi authors. In fact, several organizations, including NASA and Google X, have recently investigated this latest vision of rocket-free space flight.

It is technically possible that we can use Earth's own rotation as a means to deliver people and cargo to orbit. By constructing a tether 60,000 to 90,000 miles (96,000 to 145,000 km) long, with a counterweight at one end and the other anchored to a point along the equator, we could theoretically use Earth's approximately 1,000 miles per hour (1,609 kmh) rotational velocity to keep the tether suspended (just as a rope with a rock tied at one end remains taut as you spin it around). This tether could then act as a conduit for sending elevators up and down. Any cargo released at a high point along the elevator would remain in orbit.

While theoretically possible, there are several problems with this approach. The biggest is tensile strength: A long enough cable will break under its own weight. Steel cables falter under their own weight at about 15 miles (24 km); Kevlar can hold up at about 10 times that length, but still well short of the 60,000 miles (96,000 km) required for a space elevator. Materials engineers are placing their hopes in carbon nanotubes, tiny carbon structures that, when woven together, exhibit enormous tensile strength.

But engineers aren't yet sure how to manufacture a nanotube tether (and even if they could, it's not clear that it would be strong enough to support a space elevator). If they can build a strong enough tether, engineers will still need to overcome additional barriers, including how to avoid meteorites, space junk, and the inevitable swaying that will occur as a craft inches up the tether and drags against Earth's natural rotation.

Despite the barriers, the potential of a space elevator remains alluring. Sending a payload into orbit is currently an expensive and inefficient undertaking. If we could do away with the rocket itself, then (relatively) cheap exploration of our solar system could be within our grasp.

How Does Gravity Work?

You probably don't think about it regularly, but in the back of your mind you *know* that gravity affects your every move. You see it at work each time you watch the rain fall, throw a ball into the air, or drop a pencil. Without this omnipresent, invisible "force" you would fly off into space, along with everything else on Earth. The universe itself would become a chaotic landscape of planetary bodies aimlessly hurtling through space and often colliding.

In 1687, Isaac Newton described gravity as a force, claiming that any two objects in the universe exert a force of attraction upon each other. The Sun exerts gravity on all the planets, keeping them in orbit. Similarly, the planets exert gravity on the Sun and on all the other planets as well. The strength of these relationships is determined by the mass of the objects and the distance between them. The greater the mass of the two objects and the closer the objects are to each other, the stronger the pull of gravity.

For more than 200 years, Newton's theory of gravity went unchallenged. Then enter Albert Einstein. In early 1915, Einstein, in his groundbreaking general theory of relativity, explained that gravity is a curvature in the space-time continuum, or the "shape" of space-time. The mass of an object, Einstein claimed, causes the space around it to bend, or curve.

To understand the phenomenon, imagine a heavy ball sitting on a rubber sheet. The area occupied by the ball sags, or becomes distorted, due to the mass of the ball. Other smaller balls on the sheet roll in *toward* the heavier object because the heavy ball warps the sheet. According to Einstein, celestial bodies are not feeling the force of gravity, but rather following the natural curvature of time-space.

What is gravity and how does it work? The answer is simple: We're not quite sure. To this day, gravity's mystery hasn't been solved.

A recent alternative hypothesis to Einstein's theory of gravity states that particles called gravitons, emitted by Earth, cause a gravitational force between objects. But gravitons have never been observed and, to date, remain hypothetical. Yet another idea holds that gravity is the result of gravitational waves, generated by an interaction between two or more masses, such as the merge of two galaxies or the orbit of two black holes. Like gravitons, however, gravitational waves have never been detected.

And so the great mystery of gravity remains unsolved. And without discovering its secret, humankind may never truly comprehend how the universe works.

How Do Stars Explode?

Supernovas can occur in one of two ways: through a process of runaway nuclear fusion or through a rapid collapse of the star's core.

The first process occurs in binary star systems where at least one star is a white dwarf, a dense, aging star that can no longer support nuclear fusion. The second star can be another white dwarf, a red giant, or a main sequence star such as our own Sun that fuses hydrogen atoms to form helium atoms at its core. In either case, the white dwarf siphons off (or collides with) the mass of its companion star, reigniting nuclear fusion. Once the white dwarf reignites, it gets so hot so fast that it blows apart, outshining an entire galaxy and leaving no remnant behind.

Less luminous, though no less spectacular, are core collapse supernovas. Instead of exploding in a runaway fusion reaction, this type of supernova occurs when the star's fusion reaction grinds to a halt. For most of a star's life, it burns by fusing hydrogen atoms. This is the same process that ignites thermonuclear weapons. Eventually, the star converts most of its hydrogen into helium. The star then must fuel itself by fusing helium into carbon. If the star is heavy enough—about eight times the mass of the Sun—it will then proceed to fuse carbon into neon and helium. The star continues to fuse heavier and heavier elements until it reaches the iron phase.

It's during the iron phase that things get *really* heavy. Fusing iron does not produce more energy—in fact, iron fusion *requires* energy. Without the fusion pressure that counteracted the star's gravity, the core of the star, which is approximately the size of Earth, collapses into a space less than 10 miles (16 km) in diameter at about one-quarter light speed. When the stellar mass bounces back into space (crashing into the outer shell of the doomed star), the resultant shock wave is what we on Earth witness as a supernova.

Upon going supernova, the star may tear itself apart entirely or leave behind an extremely dense neutron star. If the core of the star is heavy enough, the supernova leaves behind one of the most mysterious objects in the known universe: a black hole.

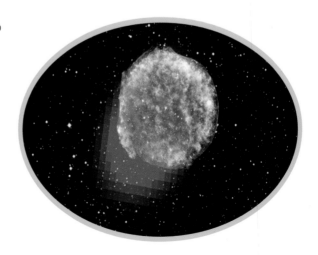

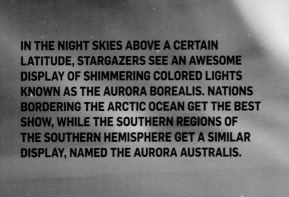

IN THE NIGHT SKIES ABOVE A CERTAIN LATITUDE, STARGAZERS SEE AN AWESOME DISPLAY OF SHIMMERING COLORED LIGHTS KNOWN AS THE AURORA BOREALIS. NATIONS BORDERING THE ARCTIC OCEAN GET THE BEST SHOW, WHILE THE SOUTHERN REGIONS OF THE SOUTHERN HEMISPHERE GET A SIMILAR DISPLAY, NAMED THE AURORA AUSTRALIS.

What Causes the Aurora Borealis?

The aurora appears as a curtain, an arc or a spiral, usually following the lines of Earth's magnetic field. Most displays are green, but strong occurrences can be red, violet, and white. For most of human history, the colors were a source of mystery. Northern cultures created legends about the lights, often associating them with life after death. The Inuit believed the spirits of their ancestors were dancing across the sky, and in Norse mythology, the aurora was a bridge of fire connecting the gods to the heavens. But by the 1880s, scientists suspected a connection between the northern lights, as they are also known, and the Sun.

The temperature above the surface of the Sun is millions of degrees Celsius, causing frequent and violent collisions among gas molecules. Electrons and protons thrown free by the collisions hurtle outward from the Sun's rotation and escape through holes in the magnetic field. Solar wind carries the charged particles, most of which deflect off Earth's magnetic field. However, near the North and South Pole, the magnetic field is weaker, allowing some particles to enter the atmosphere. When the charged particles from the Sun strike the atoms and molecules in Earth's atmosphere, they excite those atoms. An excited atom is one whose electrons move to high-energy orbits, and in the process the atom releases a particle of light, or photon. Different gases in the atmosphere give off light of different colors. Oxygen causes a green display and nitrogen produces red or blue colors. We perceive the collisions between solar particles and atmospheric gases as the northern lights.

Many tourists trek to the northern and southern poles of Earth to catch a glimpse of the auroras, now considered one of the seven wonders of the natural world. And even though science can explain the once-mysterious phenomenon, the dazzling display of lights still provokes magical thoughts of dancing ancestors and bridges to the world beyond.

Is a Holodeck Possible?

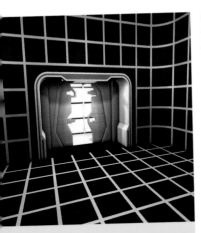

STAR TREK FANS WILL BE HAPPY TO HEAR THAT A HOLODECK IS NOT THAT FAR AWAY FROM REALITY.

The fictional simulator located on starships and starbases gave the Starfleet crew entertainment, a training mechanism, and a way to investigate mysteries. In the science fiction realm, the holodeck was a room equipped with a hologrid containing multidirectional holographic diodes, using photons and force fields to create a realistic environment. In an otherwise empty room, "solid" props and characters interacted with a holographic background capable of creating any scenario possible. Science has a different name—"tele-immersion"—for *Star Trek*'s holodeck. The

technology for this interactive virtual world is closer than you might think.

Some scientists and researchers think we will have holodecks as early as 2024. While the technology exists to create one already, it would be crude compared to the one on *Star Trek*. Taking the science fiction genre out of the equation, holodecks are simply an attempt by Hollywood and video game makers to move entertainment closer to reality. Instead of slouching on a couch during a movie or getting a thumb workout during a session of Halo, a player can maneuver a battle site while interacting with actors or run around the bases after hitting a grand slam at a New York Yankees game.

Many of the difficulties of creating a holodeck have already been solved. For example, the US Army has created a floor called an "omnidirectional treadmill" that allows users to walk around a room without running into walls. Microsoft is at the forefront of this technology, filing several patents for holodecks. The IllumiRoom, a Microsoft project, can manipulate surroundings and make furniture disappear.

Lightspace is a digital chandelier by Microsoft that can detect people and objects in a room and display images from the ceiling that cover the walls and floor. And in 2014, scientists at the University of Illinois created CAVE2, which uses 8-foot-(2.4 m)-high screens that cover 320 degrees of a room and can model global weather patterns, study the effects of drugs, and help doctors practice surgery.

Researchers have already created a 3D reality. The difficulty is creating a realistic interactive reality, where a participant can shake the hand of a coworker thousands of miles away or hit a home run that feels exactly like the real-life alternative. If science does master the holodeck, there may be significant changes in how we function. TVs, even flat-screen, HD, and "smart" devices, may become obsolete as people opt for a real-world experience. Business travel could decline if holodecks become less expensive than airplane flights and hotels. In fact, many people may opt never to leave the house again since any experience they desire can virtually drop into their living room.

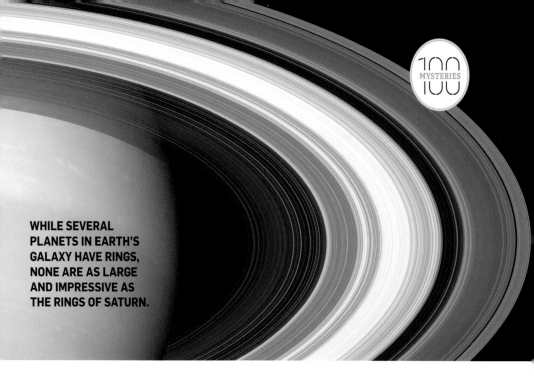

WHILE SEVERAL
PLANETS IN EARTH'S
GALAXY HAVE RINGS,
NONE ARE AS LARGE
AND IMPRESSIVE AS
THE RINGS OF SATURN.

How Did Saturn Get Its Rings?

Scientists have identified seven major rings, named for the first seven letters of the alphabet, which are made up of many more, thinner "ringlets." Although they appear solid from a distance, each ring is actually composed of individual bits of ice along with dust and fragments of space rock. These particles range in size from a tiny speck to perhaps as much as one half-mile (0.8 km) wide. The space objects that form the rings whiz around the planet at high speeds—up to thousands of miles per hour.

How Saturn got its rings is still open to debate. The NASA spacecraft Cassini, which reached Saturn in 2004, could provide answers. Cassini's research suggests that the outer E Ring is formed, in large part, from pieces of ice that break off from Enceladus, one of Saturn's known 53 moons. Closer to the planet's surface, some rings seem to be formed by particles that break off other moons when small meteoroids collide with them.

Several theories that explain how some rings formed rest on the Roche limit, which is based on a calculation first made by the 19th-century French astronomer Edouard Roche. In simple terms, the Roche limit means gravity will cause a satellite orbiting a planet to break apart if it approaches within a certain distance of the planet. The rings may be pieces of the material used to form Saturn's moon. It's possible some of the matter may have traveled within the Roche limit, the small pieces coming together in ring form. Alternatively, a small moon might have drifted within the Roche limit and Saturn's gravitational force pulled it apart, creating space debris that formed a ring.

The Cassini mission will last until at least September 2017. Scientists hope the spacecraft will provide more answers about Saturn and its rings.

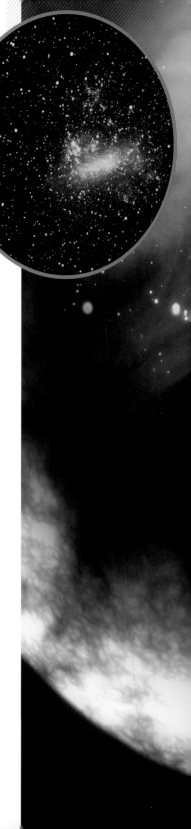

A supernova captured by the Kuiper Airborne Observatory in 1987.

Could a Supernova Wipe Out Life on Earth?

A supernova is a stellar explosion. Incredibly strong, a typical supernova can outshine an entire galaxy at its peak, ejecting a Sun's worth of stellar mass at a significant fraction of the speed of light within seconds.

And here's the harsh reality: A supernova, if it were close enough, could certainly spell the end of civilization and, perhaps, wipe out all life on Earth. As heavy radioactive elements in the ejected matter decayed, they would produce gamma rays. These gamma rays would be powerful enough to convert our ozone layer into nitrogen oxides and pure nitrogen, neither of which would protect us from the radiation of space.

The bombardment of solar and cosmic rays would destroy key parts of the ecosystem, especially plankton and coral reefs. With the collapse of these systems, the oceanic biome would likely collapse, leading to a mass extinction that would vibrate across the food chain. Given long enough exposure, the bombardment of cosmic and solar rays would threaten and, eventually, wipe out surface life—including humankind—everywhere. If any life survived, it would likely be microbes hiding deep inside Earth's crust.

As scary as this scenario is, it is also extremely unlikely. In cosmic terms, that supernova would have to be awfully close to cause any real damage. Powerful, Type Ia supernovas dim significantly beyond 75 light-years, and less powerful Type II supernovas are unlikely to cause significant damage at a distance greater than 25 light-years. Thankfully, there are no stars close enough *and* massive enough to go supernova. The nearest candidate is IK Pegasi, safely 150 light-years away (and creeping even further away from us).

Luckily for us, of the 200 to 400 million stars in the Milky Way, an average of three go supernova every century. This isn't something we have to worry about any time soon.

An artist's drawing of gamma rays hitting Earth's atmosphere, where they would eventually deplete the ozone layer, allowing in ultra-violet radiation from the Sun. This effect would damage small life-forms, disrupt the food chain and possibly bring about mass extinction.

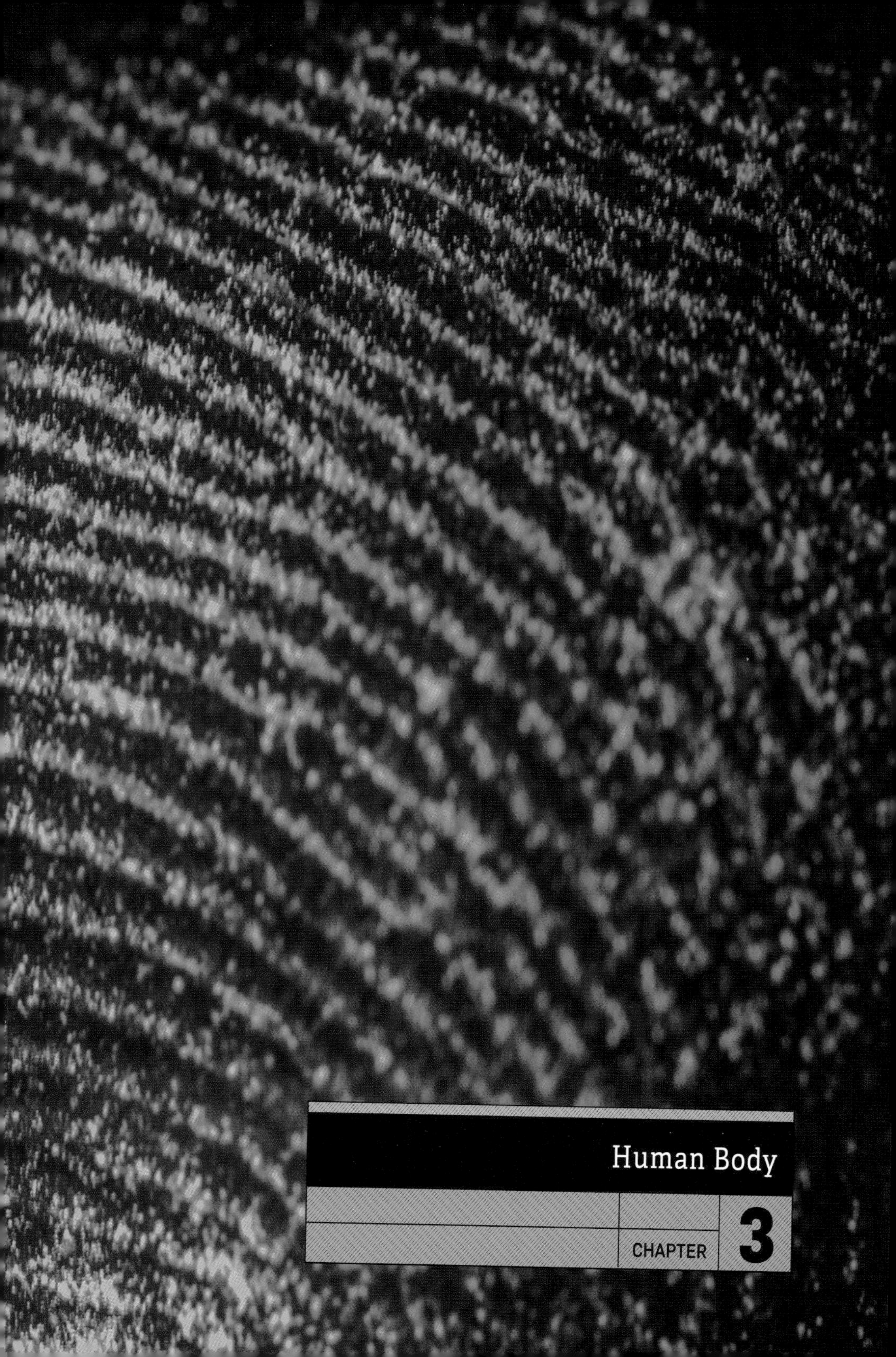

CHAPTER 3

Human Body

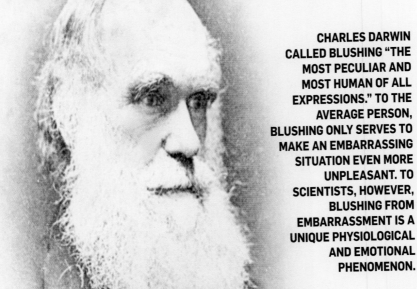

CHARLES DARWIN CALLED BLUSHING "THE MOST PECULIAR AND MOST HUMAN OF ALL EXPRESSIONS." TO THE AVERAGE PERSON, BLUSHING ONLY SERVES TO MAKE AN EMBARRASSING SITUATION EVEN MORE UNPLEASANT. TO SCIENTISTS, HOWEVER, BLUSHING FROM EMBARRASSMENT IS A UNIQUE PHYSIOLOGICAL AND EMOTIONAL PHENOMENON.

Why Do We Blush?

We understand the chemistry, the physical process, of blushing, but *why* we blush remains an elusive mystery to researchers. The physiology of blushing is quite simple. When you're embarrassed, your adrenal glands and certain neurons of the central nervous system release the hormone adrenaline. The general effect of adrenaline is to prepare the body for the "fight or flight" response: increasing heart rate and blood pressure, enlarging the pupil of the eye, and increasing blood flow and oxygen to the muscles, among other consequences.

When you experience the stress of embarrassment, adrenaline causes the veins in your face to dilate, or widen, allowing more blood to flow through them. The increased presence of blood in your face makes your cheeks feel warm and creates the reddened look that signals to others you're embarrassed.

Blushing triggered by embarrassment is a one-of-a-kind phenomenon: It is exclusive to humans, and it does not happen anywhere else in your body. Why is this reaction so specific? Why have humans developed this unique response to embarrassment?

Science does not yet have all the answers, but recent studies suggest that blushing serves a functional purpose, having evolved as a means of establishing social relationships. In a study conducted in 2009, a team of Dutch psychologists led by Corine Kijk, Peter de Jong, and Madelon Peters discovered that blushing "serves to signal the actor's genuine regret or remorse over a wrongdoing." In effect, blushing functions as a nonverbal "I'm sorry" for committing an embarrassing act or breaching a societal norm. It thereby mitigates "the negative social impression that was caused by the infraction." According to the researchers, your blushing makes others perceive you have acknowledged your blunder and learned from your mistake.

The Dutch study concluded with some helpful advice: "Our results showed that in the context of transgressions and mishaps, blushing is a helpful bodily signal with face-saving properties. It seems therefore unwise to hide the blush or to try not to blush in these types of contexts."

What Is the Evolutionary Purpose of Tickling?

You probably know that you can't tickle yourself. And although you might be able to tickle a total stranger, your brain strongly discourages you from doing something so socially awkward.

These facts offer insight into tickling's evolutionary purpose, says Robert R. Provine, a neuroscientist at the University of Maryland and the author of the book *Laughter: A Scientific Investigation*. Tickling, he says, is a mechanism for social bonding between close companions, helping to forge relationships between family members and friends.

Laughter in response to tickling kicks in during the first few months of life. "It's one of the first forms of communication between babies and their caregivers," Provine says. Parents learn to tickle a baby only as long as she laughs in response. When the baby starts fussing instead, they stop. The face-to-face activity also opens the door for other interactions.

Children enthusiastically tickle each other, which some scientists say not only inspires peer bonding but also might hone reflexes and self-defense skills. In 1984, psychiatrist Donald Black of the University of Iowa noted that many ticklish parts of the body, such as the neck and the ribs, are also the most vulnerable in combat. He inferred that children learn to protect those parts during tickle fights, a relatively safe activity.

Tickling while horsing around also may have given rise to laughter itself. "The 'ha ha' of human laughter almost certainly evolved from the 'pant pant' of rough-and-tumble human play," says Provine, who bases that conclusion on observations of panting in apes that tickle each other, such as chimpanzees and orangutans. In adulthood, our response to tickling trails off around the age of 40. At that point, the fun stops; for reasons unknown, tickling seems to be mainly for the young.

Why Do We Yawn?

We all do it, and even some animals as well, when we're ready to go to sleep and sometimes when we awaken. We do it when we're bored, and we might do it under stress. We can even catch it from another person, but as common as yawning is, scientists have struggled to explain why we yawn. Recent research suggests some possible explanations.

One theory among chasmologists—scientists who study yawning—is that the act is a form of social behavior. Contagious yawns are quite common—about half the people who see or hear a yawn will yawn too. Christian Hess of the University of Bern in Switzerland thinks the easy spread of yawns helped early humans learn to synchronize their desire to go to sleep and awake at the same time, allowing them to coordinate their daily activities.

Maryland psychologist Robert Provine is one chasmologist who thinks a yawn stirs up our brains. So when we're sleepy, a yawn wakes us up, and if we need mental sharpness to deal with stress, the yawn provides it. As part of this theory, the yawn could be stimulating the flow of cerebrospinal fluid, which clears out chemicals in the brain that make us sleepy. The brain-stimulating yawn also has a social component: Provine says a contagious yawn spawned by stress could signal members of a group to prepare for danger.

Instead of synchronizing bedtimes or sweeping out unwanted chemicals, a yawn could regulate temperature. That's the theory of Andrew Gallup, a psychologist at the State University of New York at Oneonta. Basically, he says, "We yawn to cool our brains." Yawning increases the flow of blood to the brain, forcing out warm blood that has gathered there. Simultaneously, the yawn brings cooling air into the body through the mouth and nose. A typical yawn, Gallup said, can lower the temperature in the brain by 0.2 degrees Fahrenheit (-17.67 °C). A string of yawns can lower it by half a degree more.

Working off this theory, Gallup and some scientists in Vienna tested the incidence of contagious yawning at different temperatures. Their results suggested that contagious yawning most often takes place when the outside temperature is in a "thermal window" of around 68 degrees Fahrenheit (20 degrees Celsius). Yawning decreases when the outside temperature and body temperature are close, or when it's cold outside.

THE NUMBER OF SCHOOL-AGE CHILDREN WITH PEANUT ALLERGIES HAS DOUBLED IN THE PAST DECADE. YET SCIENTISTS HAVE NOT IDENTIFIED WHAT MAKES THE LEGUME SUCH A THREAT OR WHY THE ALLERGY HAS BECOME SO PREVALENT.

Why Are Peanut Allergies on the Rise?

Typically, the immune system treats peanuts as safe, but some scientists believe that early and heavy exposure to peanut-laden products might cause the immune system to misidentify them as dangerous. This theory is strengthened by the fact that 8 out of 10 allergic kids have a reaction the first time they eat a peanut, indicating a previous indirect exposure, possibly even in the womb or through breast milk.

Theories about peanut allergies abound and most involve an overactive immune system. "We have done such a good job of eliminating the threats that the immune system is supposed to manage that it's looking for something to do," says Anne Muñoz-Furlong, former CEO of the nonprofit Food Allergy and Anaphylaxis Network. Parents today feed their kids a lot of ready-made snacks, many of which contain peanuts or their derivatives. "We're bombarding the immune system with these [food-based] allergens, so it's attacking those instead." Indeed, food allergies in general are on the rise.

But peanuts seem to trigger especially violent immune reactions. This might be because they contain several proteins not found in most other foods, posits Robert Wood, an allergy specialist at Johns Hopkins University, and the structure of these proteins can stimulate a strong immune response. Research suggests that roasting peanuts, as American companies do, might alter the proteins' shape, making them an even bigger target. Allergy rates are lower in China, where it's customary to boil peanuts, which damages the proteins less. (It's worth noting, though, that China is also more polluted, so people's immune systems might be concentrating on traditional threats.)

Or maybe it's all the time indoors. Children who spend little time outdoors tend to be deficient in D, Wood says, so their bodies might mislabel peanut proteins as dangerous. Parents looking to protect their kids might consider sending them outside—and not washing their hands when they come home.

100% GUARANTEE NUT FREE 100% GUARANTEE

What Is a Memory?

Scientists say there could be a reason why you don't remember what you ate for breakfast last week but can vividly describe your first day of kindergarten. Emotional meaning attached to a memory makes it stick in a way that everyday details can't. But memories aren't just about the past. They help us learn and make decisions about the future.

Neuroscientists do not completely understand the physical representation of memories in the brain. Neurons, or brain cells, communicate with each other through electrochemical pathways. An electrical impulse travels down the outgoing branch called an axon, where it stimulates fingers known as dendrites at the end, releasing neurotransmitters. These tiny molecules send messages that incoming branches pick up. The space between these branches is called a synapse.

The reconstruction of a past experience happens through synchronous firing of neurons involved in the original experience. A memory is not a static entity but a unique pattern of activity that can shift or migrate between different parts of the brain. It is like a jigsaw puzzle that assembles throughout various areas of the brain, rather than a video clip stored as a whole file. Short-term memories do not "stick" in the synapse, and long-term memories might be distorted when they reassemble.

One of the most important attributes of memory is our ability to learn. When we learn or recall information, we use memory to retrieve the idea we have learned. Every time you eat, drive a car or read a book, you are remembering learned traits. New technology called optogenetics uses light beams to excite or silence a targeted group of neurons in the brain, helping scientists study and perhaps control memories. It may be possible to open up a pathway to selectively implant memories or erase certain memories altogether. For people with amnesia or severe emotional trauma, that will be a moment worth remembering.

DO YOU EVER WONDER WHY YOU FORGOT WHAT YOU WERE LOOKING FOR AS SOON AS YOU SET OFF TO FIND SOMETHING? OR WHY YOU CAN'T RECALL THE ENDING OF A BOOK YOU READ LAST YEAR?

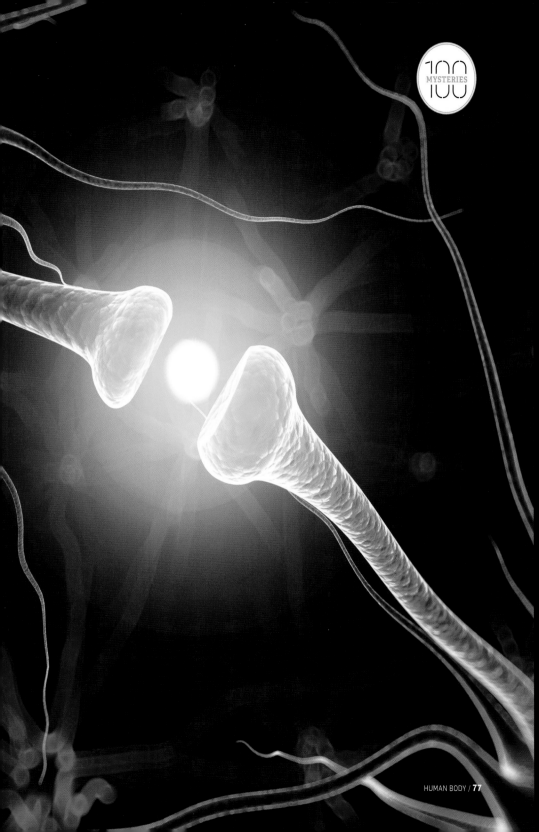

Why Do
We Dream?

Dreams remain one of the most mysterious aspects of the human experience. Diviners, doctors and scientists have pondered the phenomenon of dreaming for centuries. Despite a plethora of competing theories that attempt to explain why we dream, no particular idea has achieved a consensus among researchers.

The classic exploration of dreams—the one that pop culture invokes time and time again—is Freud's *The Interpretation of Dreams*, published in 1899. The founding psychotherapist believed that dreams are our mechanism for living out our most aggressive, carnal desires—the urges that we're not allowed to act on in real life—so that we don't go insane from repressing them during the daytime. Though the field of psychoanalysis has largely moved on from Freud, our need to ascribe meaning to our dreams and to master our subconscious renders the Freudian approach compelling to this day.

On the other hand, minimalist sleep researchers propose that dreams are devoid of any objective meaning. Harvard psychiatrists J. Allan Hobson and Robert McCarley generated a firestorm of controversy in 1977 when they argued that dreams are nothing but the side effects of spontaneous activity taking place in the synapses in the brain stem during sleep. In other words, our dreams (and the meanings that we ascribe to them) are nothing but our subjective attempt to reconcile those mental stimuli.

In between these two extremes are a slew of theories that frame dreams as functionally, if not necessarily psychologically, important. Experiments show that dreams help subjects solve problems and puzzles that researchers posed to them before dream sleep. This finding

jibes with theories that dreaming is crucial to memory storage, information processing, and cleaning out the synaptic garbage that the brain collects as a result of its normal operation. Other research indicates that dreams play an important role in stress relief, a theory supported by a decrease in stress hormones during dream sleep.

Psychologist Deirdre Barrett, also of Harvard, focuses on our least favorite subset of dreams: nightmares. She claims that even these unwelcome dreams once posed the important evolutionary function of focusing attention on the dangers our ancestors faced in everyday life. All these functionalist hypotheses suggest that dreams developed as a function of the mammalian brain in order to fulfill an evolutionary purpose. What that purpose is remains a puzzle. Perhaps we should sleep on it?

Theodore
Roosevelt,
ca. 1919

"Laughter is the closest distance between two people."

— VICTOR BORGE

Why Do We Laugh?

We hear laughter all the time—from a giggle to a snicker to a full-blown belly laugh. Laughter is undoubtedly a common human behavior, yet it has vexed scientists for centuries. To this day, the question "Why do we laugh?" remains a much-debated topic.

An apparent answer to the question would be that we laugh when we think something is funny. In this case, laughter—the contractions of facial muscles accompanied by an audible sound ranging from a quiet titter to a loud cackle—would be the physiological response to humor. This might be the *apparent* answer, but it's not the full story. The reasons that we need this response are more complicated than you'd think.

As it turns out, studying laughter is no joking matter, according to Robert R. Provine, professor of psychology and neuroscience at the University of Maryland. Provine, the author of the book *Laughter: A Scientific Investigation*, has conducted numerous studies on mirth. "Most laughter is not in response to jokes or humor," says Provine. Most of it occurs in ordinary conversations, in which nothing at all humorous transpires. In one of his most-publicized studies, Provine observes that laughs can be elicited by a variety of non-joke statements such as "Hey, John, where ya been?" or "How did you do on the test?"

"It is about relationships between people," claims Provine. "We don't decide to laugh at these moments. Our brain makes the decision for us. These curious 'ha ha ha's' are bits of the social glue that bond relationships."

Provine believes that human laughter predated human speech by millions of years.

Before speech, laughter was a primary form of communication. "Laughter," says Provine, "evolved from the panting behavior of our ancient primate ancestors." Apes and other animals, including rats, make "laugh-like" sounds and high-pitched vocalizations while playing, but it would be erroneous to equate them with human laughter. However, "When we laugh, we're often communicating playful intent. So laughter has a bonding function between individuals in a group," says Provine.

While most laughter is a positive behavior, it can have negative intent. Pointing out one social function of laughter, Provine cites the difference between "laughing with" and "laughing at" someone. "People who laugh at others may be trying to force them to conform or casting them out of the group," he says.

While studies have yet to prove that laughter is the best medicine or has any appreciable degree of health benefits, for that matter, Provine notes, "If we enjoy laughing, isn't that reason enough to laugh? Do you really need a prescription?"

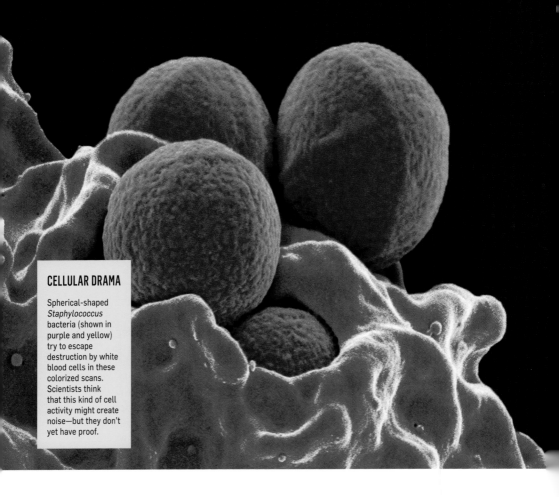

CELLULAR DRAMA

Spherical-shaped *Staphylococcus* bacteria (shown in purple and yellow) try to escape destruction by white blood cells in these colorized scans. Scientists think that this kind of cell activity might create noise—but they don't yet have proof.

Do Cells Make Noise?

You have to listen very, very closely, but yes, cells produce a symphony of sounds. Although they won't win a Grammy anytime soon, the various audio blips produced by cells give scientists insight into cellular biomechanics and could even be used to help detect cancer.

Researchers at the University of California at Los Angeles studying brewer's yeast discovered that the yeast's cell walls vibrate 1,000 times per second. These motions are too slight and fast to be caught on video, but when converted into sound, they create what the scientists describe as a high-pitched scream. It's about the same frequency as two octaves above middle C on a piano, but it's not loud enough to hear with the naked ear. "I think if you listened to it for too long, you would go mad," says biological physicist Andrew Pelling, at the University of Ottawa. Pelling and Jim Gimzewski, a professor of biochemistry at UCLA, theorize that molecular motors that transport proteins around the yeast cell cause the walls to vibrate.

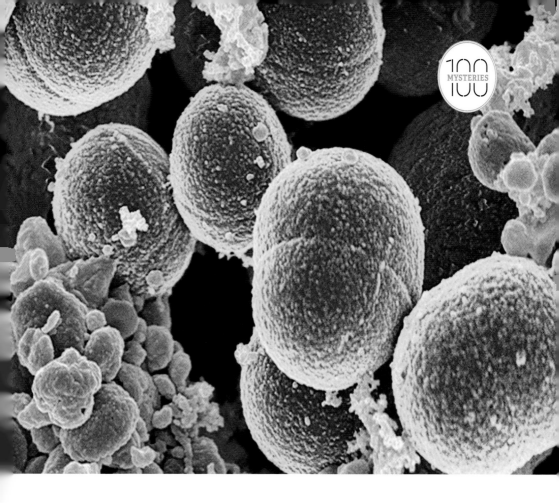

It's a little harder to get sound out of a human cell than from a yeast cell: So far, scientists have not observed mammalian cells that audibly shimmy on their own, at least in part because animal cells' wiggly membranes are less likely to vibrate than the sturdy cell walls of yeast and plants. But human cells certainly squeal when zapped with light, a trait that could be surprisingly useful for medical science, particularly cancer research.

When Richard Snook and Peter Gardner, biologists at the University of Manchester in England, blasted human prostate cells with infrared light, their microphones picked up thousands of simultaneous notes generated by the cells. Through statistical analysis of these sounds—which are created as the cells rapidly heat up and cool down, causing vibrations in the air molecules directly above them—Snook and Gardner can differentiate between normal and cancerous cells. "The difference between a healthy cell and a cancer cell is like listening to two very large orchestras playing their instruments all at the same time," Gardner says. "But in the cancerous orchestra, the tuba is horribly out of tune." Gardner is fine-tuning the technique in hopes of replacing current, unreliable pre-biopsy prostate-cancer tests. His ultimate goal is to reduce the number of prostate biopsies performed, 75 percent of which come back negative.

How Does the Brain Work?

The main functional unit of the brain is a type of nerve cell called the neuron, of which the human brain possesses roughly 100 billion. The human body contains three types of neurons, each different in function. Sensory neurons carry signals from the outside world into the central nervous system. Motor neurons carry signals from the central nervous system to muscles and glands. Interneurons form a connection between other neurons; they are neither sensory nor motor. Each sensation, memory, thought, and movement we experience is the result of electrochemical signals that pass through neurons. The brain's ability to function is the result of the 24/7 activity of neurons.

YOUR BRAIN— THE 3-POUND (1.3 KG) BLOB OF NEURONS, CHEMICALS, HORMONES, WATER, AND FAT SITTING IN YOUR SKULL—IS THE MOST COMPLEX PART OF THE HUMAN BODY.

The human brain consists of the brain stem, the cerebellum, the cerebrum, and the limbic system.

The **BRAIN STEM** contains the medulla, which regulates heart rate and breathing; the pons, which links to the cerebellum to help with movement and posture, as well as creating a certain level of consciousness necessary for sleep; and the midbrain, which helps regulate body movement, hearing, and vision.

The **CEREBELLUM**, often called "the little brain," allows the body to move properly, controlling functions such as posture, balance, and coordination.

The **CEREBRUM** is the largest part of the brain, and responsible for most of its functions. It is divided into four sections: (1) the frontal lobe, which controls, among other things, intellect, judgment, creative thought, problem solving, muscle movements, smell, and personality; (2) the parietal lobe, which focuses on comprehension and monitors visual functions, reading, and tactile sensation; (3) the temporal lobe, which controls visual and auditory memories; and (4) the occipital lobe, which is responsible for processing visual information. The cerebrum is split into a left and a right hemisphere, connected by neurons that pass information from one side to the other.

The **LIMBIC SYSTEM** contains glands that help relay hormonal responses in the body. The amygdala is responsible for the response and memory of emotions, especially fear. The hippocampus helps process long-term memory and emotional responses. The hypothalamus controls hunger, thirst, and body temperature, while the thalamus helps control attention span and monitors information in and out of the brain to track bodily sensations, such as pain.

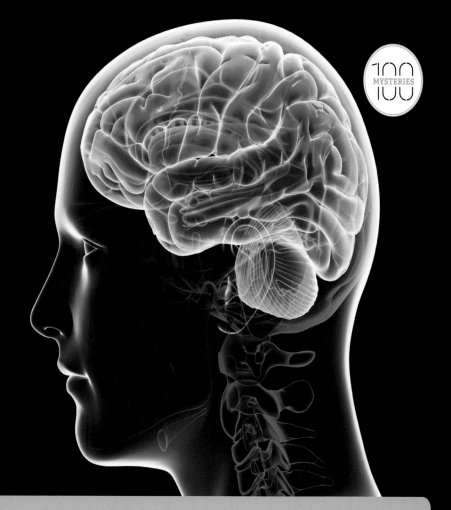

The regions of the brain frequently work independently, but sometimes different regions work together to perform a task. For example, several regions in the brain function cooperatively to allow us to read. MRI brain scans show that the ability to sound out printed words is a function of a part of the parietal lobe, while making connections with a new word and sound is associated with the cerebellum and hippocampus. The ability to read out loud quickly appears to be a function of several brain locations.

Despites centuries of scientific study, however, we are at still at a loss to explain many of the human brain's mysteries.

Among the unsolved puzzles scientists are trying to unravel are the following:

How are memories stored and retrieved?

How do brains make sound predictions about the world?

What does "intelligence" mean in biological terms?

Getting a stronger grip on the functioning of the brain could have enormous ramifications. According to Norman Weinberger, a neuroscientist at the University of California, Irvine, "If we understand the brain, we will understand both its capacities and its limits for thought, emotions, reasoning, love, and every other aspect of human life."

What Is Emotion?

Although feelings of love, hate, anger, and joy are common responses for most people, emotions have always been thought to be subjective feelings that vary depending on the person. For example, two people engaging in an argument will have different levels of response and may experience different sensations. Emotions are a difficult field of study for scientists because their complexity and uniqueness make them nearly impossible to measure.

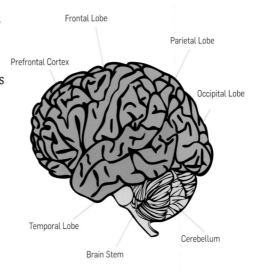

Frontal Lobe

Parietal Lobe

Prefrontal Cortex

Occipital Lobe

Temporal Lobe

Cerebellum

Brain Stem

Neuroscientists studying the brain have narrowed down the areas most active during an emotional response. Feelings of happiness and pleasure are linked to the prefrontal cortex, while anger, fear, and other negative emotions are linked to the amygdala. Expressive behavior, such as smiling or laughing, is the outward sign of emotion. Most people also have physiological responses to emotion, such as turning red, a pounding heart, or adrenaline release. Different chemicals in the brain control the level of emotion a person experiences. At any moment, dozens of neurotransmitters, or chemical messengers, travel through individual cells throughout the entire brain. If a person is in danger, the brain releases stress hormones, flooding certain regions with adrenaline. These measurable signs of emotion differ between individuals, however, again suggesting that emotion is subjective. But according to a new study by Cornell neuroscientist Adam Anderson, that is not exactly the case. Two people who have a

similar reaction to a sunset share a similar pattern of activity in the orbitofrontal cortex, a region of the prefrontal cortex. "Despite how personal our feelings feel, the evidence suggests our brains use a standard code to speak the same emotional language," Anderson explains.

Whether emotions are objective or subjective, scientists are still not entirely sure why we feel what we feel, or why we express it in particular ways. Anderson calls emotions "the last frontier of neuroscience." Most people consider emotions a necessary part of being human. They add depth to the human experience. Empathy, in particular, is an important by-product of emotion. Scientists trace the feeling of empathy to mirror neurons, cells in the brain that fire when we see someone else in a situation that we can imagine ourselves in. People with autism spectrum disorders have difficulty showing empathy, and researchers believe that a better understanding of the physical processes behind emotion can solve these and other psychological disorders.

Is It True That You Use Only 10 Percent of Your Brain?

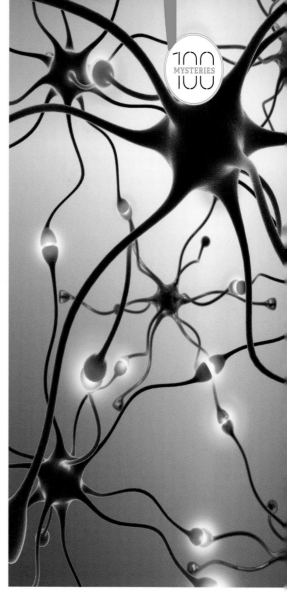

Historians have traced the earliest reference to this rumor back to the beginning of the 20th century, when it was perpetuated by self-help gurus promising to expand people's mental abilities. However, like so many things hucksters have told us, the brain claim is false. "There's no question," says Marcus Raichle, a neurologist and professor of radiology at Washington University in St. Louis, "you're using every little bit of this thing."

Even when you're sleeping or just watching TV, your brain is burning a surprising amount of energy for its size. Although your brain constitutes about 2 percent of your body weight, it accounts for 20 percent of the total energy that your body consumes.

Scientists know that most of your brain's energy is used for basic upkeep and communication between neurons. The rest, they speculate, might go toward preparing the brain to receive information by making predictions based on past experiences. For example, instead of scanning your entire fridge each time you want to grab some milk, you can reach directly for the shelf where you last left it—because your brain is working hard to remind you of its location and shoot your hand in that direction. This preprocessing helps you deal with the enormous amount of detail you encounter every day.

You can be certain that all of your brain is working hard, even when you're not thinking hard. "We should back away from the notion that the only thing the brain is doing is sitting around waiting for something to happen," Raichle says. "Every piece of it is running full-tilt all the time."

What Causes Déjà Vu?

Few of us ever experience significant supernatural phenomena, but 60 to 80 percent of us do report having the strange sensation that we've already experienced something that we consciously *know* we are actually experiencing for the first time. Like feeling you've had the same exact conversation with someone before. Or walking into a room you have never been in before, and sensing that you've been there in the past.

If you've ever had feelings such as these, you've experienced déjà vu, the sense of having experienced something previously, although it is, in reality, entirely new. *Déjà vu* comes from the French term meaning "already seen."

The phenomenon of déjà vu is difficult to study because it occurs only briefly and without notice, and it fades quickly. In addition, there is no physical manifestation of the experience, leaving scientists little to work with other than self-reported descriptions. So although researchers have been studying déjà vu for more than 100 years and theories to explain it abound, there is no single conclusive explanation for why it happens or what processes are involved in its occurrence.

Many modern researchers believe déjà vu is a memory-based cerebral experience. The precise interplay of brain functions, however, remains uncertain. One prevalent hypothesis, called the cellphone theory, or divided attention, proposes that a brief distraction might explain the feeling that we have experienced something before. Imagine walking down a street while chatting with a friend on your cellphone. Engrossed in your conversation, you pass a brand-new restaurant for the first time, your brain subliminally, shallowly acknowledging the new eatery. Moments later, when the conversation has ended and you focus your complete attention on your surroundings, you become fully conscious of the restaurant—and are struck with a feeling of déjà vu. What's happened? Your brain, while observant of all your surroundings, had been working below conscious awareness, and when you returned your full attention to the restaurant, you got the feeling you were familiar with it. In fact, you were: You just hadn't been paying attention.

Another hypothesis, the hologram theory, proposes that some feature in our environment, such as a sight or a sound that resembles a distant memory, triggers the brain to create a complete scene of the déjà vu experience. As you study a small portion of a painting you've never seen before, for instance, a distant memory surfaces from deep within your brain. According to the hologram theory, this occurs because memories are stored in a form like holograms, and with holograms you need only one fragment in order to see the full picture. Your brain identifies the portion of the painting with the past memory, perhaps a similar painting or a comparable photograph you've seen. However, instead of remembering that you've seen something similar in the past, your brain recalls the old memory without identifying it, leaving you with a sense of familiarity with the painting—your déjà vu experience—but no recollection of the original memory.

Researchers hope that advances in brain imaging technology will allow us to better understand how the human brain works and to pinpoint exactly how the déjà vu phenomenon occurs.

Is the Y Chromosome Doomed?

Humans store their genes in 23 pairs of chromosomes, 22 of which are identically matched. The 23rd is a two-sided biological coin— twin Xs mean you're female; an X and a Y, male. Chromosome pairs often trade bits of DNA in a process called recombination, the purpose of which is to keep genes functioning properly.

The Y chromosome is small in comparison to other chromosomes, containing only 27 unique genes as compared to thousands on others. A result of natural selection, this indicates that it is stripped down to its essential purpose.

Talk of men's path toward extinction began in the late 1990s when it was discovered that the human Y chromosome, which is stumpy compared with the X, does not share enough genetic material with the X to practice recombination. Left without a way to renew damaged genes, the Y would continue to degrade and would eventually disappear, geneticists announced. They slapped an expiration date on the male half of the species of sometime in the next 5 to 10 million years.

To get a perspective on this prediction, scientists looked to our closest genetic relatives—the chimps. Because humans and chimpanzees shared a common ancestor 6 million years ago, geneticist David Page of the Whitehead Institute for Biomedical Research in Cambridge, Massachusetts, studied how the chimp Y chromosome and its human Y counterpart have evolved differently in the intervening years. What he found surprised him: The chimp Y chromosome is far more degraded than the human Y chromosome.

Page and his colleagues speculate that chimps' promiscuity—females mate with multiple partners—has led to enhancement of the Y genes that produce sperm, to the detriment of other genes. Among chimps, "there are sperm wars going on. Each male is trying to pass his own genes down," says Jennifer Hughes, who coauthored the study. Neglected, the chimp Y chromosome's nonreproductive genes have declined.

The Whitehead Institute scientists think that although the human Y chromosome also lost genes at first, in recent eons it has been relatively stable. The human Y has eluded the chimp Y's fate, they suggest, because humans are largely monogamous. Human sperm don't face the same competition as chimps', so there isn't as much pressure on the human Y to produce good sperm.

Not all geneticists are convinced that the human Y has stopped deteriorating. Jenny A. Marshall Graves of the Australian National University in Canberra believes that the Y chromosome's days are numbered. "The human Y has been degenerating since it was born, 300 million years ago," she says. And so the controversy continues. Rest assured, though; the Y chromosome—and the guys—will be around for a while.

Do Men and Women Have Different Brains?

While society has continued to move away from the myth of sex and gender as "binary" scientific studies have shown there are some differences between brains of cisgender men and cisgender women. Anecdotally, men tend to gravitate toward math and science disciplines, while women lean toward excellence at language.

To study brain connectivity, researchers use a type of scan called DTI, a technique that maps the diffusion of water molecules within brain tissue, tracing fiber pathways that connect different regions of the brain. Women's brains contain about 9.5 times as much white matter, the substance that connects various parts of the brain. The bridge of nerve tissue that connects the right and left side of the brain is stronger in women, perhaps explaining why they are more equipped for multitasking. Women activate both the left and right hemispheres when listening to language. The frontal and temporal areas of the cortex are bigger and better organized, helping women score better on attention, facial recognition, and social cognition. Women are faster and more accurate when identifying emotions and seem better at controlling them.

In contrast, men tend to focus on a single issue and excel at it. Studies of men's brains show fewer connections between the right and left hemispheres. Men's brains are about 10 percent larger than women's brains and contain about 6.5 times more gray matter, or "thinking matter." Men appear to be better at special processing, meaning that they are more aware of where they sit on a map. They rely on the hippocampus to place where they are, whereas women tend to rely on landmarks. But it's not all good news—men are more susceptible to attention deficit disorder (ADD) and lack of impulse control.

Despite these findings, many studies show fewer differences between the brains of men and women than previously believed. Moreover, many studies have shown that brains do not typically adhere to "male" and "female" patterns, but are more often unique blends. "All of these things have overlapping distributions. There are many women with better-than-average spatial skills, and men with good writing skills," says David Geary, professor of psychological services at the University of Missouri. Some researchers argue that exercising one's brain, especially at a young age, can enhance areas of difficulty. Most importantly, men and women perform equally well on broad measures of cognitive ability.

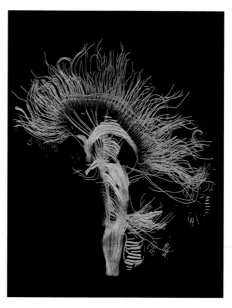

Why Do We Sleep?

Catch 40 winks, nod off, hit the hay— we all sleep, spending roughly one-third of our lives doing it. Why humans need to sleep, though, is a question scientists still haven't answered.

What's obvious is that without sleep, we lack energy and our thinking process can become muddled. Sleep deprivation can also lead to accidents on the road or at work, various health ailments, decreased sex drive, and symptoms of depression, among other problems. And while reported cases of human beings directly dying from lack of sleep are rare, the physiological changes that occur from sleep deprivation can be more detrimental, and possibly fatal, than going without food.

Over the years, scientists have advanced several theories about the role sleep plays in human health. One theory suggests that sleep, and the conservation of energy that goes with it, helped humans and other species evolve. Using less energy for part of the day lowers the demand for food. For humans, sleeping at night meant they were conserving energy during the time when it would be hardest to find food. Some scientists see a link between this theory and one called the adaptive or evolutionary theory. Early humans saw the value of staying inactive at night in order to avoid drawing the attention of nocturnal predators. This prolonged inactivity evolved into sleep.

Another explanation for why we sleep is the restorative theory. During sleep, parts of the body restore themselves—tissues are repaired, hormones are released, proteins in brain cells are synthesized.

Neuroscientists talk about the brain's plasticity—its ability to modify its internal structure as it encounters changes in the environment or the body itself. Sleep seems to play a role in this plasticity, as neurons forge new pathways during those hours, especially in young people. While asleep, the brain also processes memories so that they can be drawn upon for future use. Research suggests that the neural connections that create memories strengthen when we sleep.

A more recent theory about the importance of sleep has called it a "biological dishwasher." During sleep, the

brain flushes out waste products that accumulate there during the day. One of these substances is adenosine, which is found in all cells. In the brain it's created during neural activity, and as it accumulates it makes us feel sleepy. When we actually do sleep, the body flushes the adenosine out of the brain,

helping us feel revived when we wake.

In 2013, this idea of sleep and biological cleansing received a boost from research done on mice. Their brain cells shrank while they slept, creating pathways for spinal fluid to pass through. The fluid flowed ten times faster during sleep than when the mice were awake.

The flow of the spinal fluid helped carry away the brain's waste products as well as proteins that can harm the brain when too many of them accumulate there.

Today, scientists don't agree that any one theory explains why we sleep. They continue to probe what exactly happens in the brain when we grab some shut-eye.

Why Do We Hiccup?

If you've ever chugged a carbonated drink, felt overwhelmed by fear, or experienced a bloated stomach, you might have hiccuped soon after. These and other actions and conditions can trigger hiccups, and sometimes they start for no clear reason at all.

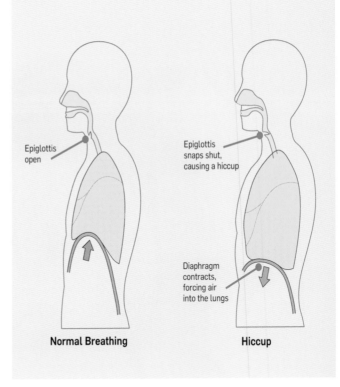

Epiglottis open

Normal Breathing

Epiglottis snaps shut, causing a hiccup

Diaphragm contracts, forcing air into the lungs

Hiccup

Hiccups—singultus in the medical world—occurs during the breathing process when the diaphragm breaks out of its normal rhythm of moving up and down and suddenly contracts involuntarily. When this happens, air rushes down the throat and hits the vocal cords as they shut, creating the "hic" sound.

Although hiccups are a common occurrence, they don't seem to have any real biological purpose. As to why they happen, one theory is that the nerves that control the vocal cords and the diaphragm get out of whack for some reason scientists don't understand. The malfunction could result from damage or irritation to those nerves. From an evolutionary standpoint, hiccups may have once been helpful in swallowing food or dislodging a stuck morsel.

Humans start hiccuping very early: A fetus may hiccup in the womb. Some scientists think hiccups could help developing infants prepare for breathing once they leave the womb. Whatever their purpose, fetal hiccups are common.

Hiccups *can* be a sign of illness or hurt us on their own. Although most outbreaks last for only seconds or minutes, some people have endured nonstop hiccups for days or weeks. In those extreme cases, a person could develop problems with eating, sleeping, or breathing, and doctors recommend seeking treatment if hiccups last more than 48 hours. In 2007, a Florida teenager made the news when she hiccuped for more than five weeks straight, sometimes 50 times per minute. She couldn't go to school and had trouble sleeping, and doctors couldn't explain what caused this severe hiccuping bout. The girl received various medical treatments, including acupuncture, but it isn't clear whether the hiccups responded to the treatment or finally just stopped on their own.

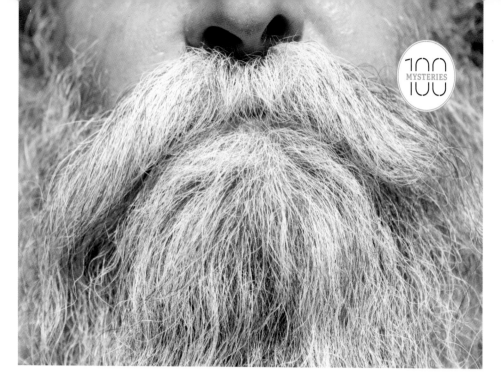

Why Aren't (Most) Humans Furry?

Ever since Darwin first made headlines, scientists have been pondering why humans lost their natural coats as they evolved from apes. The theories range from lice to cannibalism.

The traditional theory—refined by scientists over the past 40 years—proposes that humans gradually became furless in order to withstand the brutal heat of the African savanna or to prevent overheating while chasing prey.

One alternative idea, put forth in 2003 by evolutionary biologist Mark Pagel of the University of Reading in England, is that as humans learned to keep warm by making clothing and building shelters, they no longer needed heavy body hair. This hairlessness prevented parasites, such as mites and ticks, from sticking to their bodies. Avoiding parasites led to healthier humans, Pagel posits, and because there's nothing as attractive as a bug-free hominid, hairlessness became a desirable feature in a mate, and natural selection drove the hairier folks into extinction.

In 2006, developmental psychologist Judith Rich Harris suggested a far more gruesome mechanism. As humans became hairless as a result of chance mutations, they split geographically from their hairy cousins. Once hairlessness was in style, any hairy baby born to a hairless tribe was abandoned. As hairlessness became the norm, a thick fur coat would have become so rare that hairy humans would have been seen as animals and hunted for food. The days before waxing were savage indeed.

What Is the Science Behind Love?

H elen Fisher is a biological anthropologist at Rutgers University in New Jersey and a prominent researcher of the science behind the emotion of love. She divides the process of how romantic, sexual couples experience love into three stages—each driven by corresponding hormones that play a part in directing their actions. First, two people who experience sexual attraction meet and feel sexual excitement for each other. In both people, testosterone is usually at play. Once they establish this attraction, the two often begin to feel an emotional, romantic love for each other. (There are also many different types of love and romance, such as asexual, allosexual, aromantic, platonic, and others experienced with and without sexual attraction.)

Working in the brain at this point is dopamine, which creates the emotional high of being in love. At the same time, other chemicals, including adrenaline, make the heart pound a little harder when the beloved is around.

The third stage, sustaining a loving relationship, is possible in part because of oxytocin. Scientists have studied the role this hormone plays in creating a bond between a mother and her child. Oxytocin also helps build the bonds of attachment between partners. Studies done by Beate Ditzen at the University of Zurich indicate that the hormone makes lovers more able to express their feelings and be supportive of each other. Oxytocin also reduces cortisol, a hormone that stimulates stress. Genes may play a part in how receptive someone is to oxytocin.

Once this type of couple begins their relationship, their bodies respond in particular ways. These types of partners with successful, lasting relationships show fewer signs of stress (measured by the fight-or-flight syndrome scale) when conversing, while couples facing rocky times show stress even in mundane conversations. This stress can affect the immune and endocrine systems, raising the risk of disease.

Fisher believes, however, that biology alone does not determine whom we love and whether the relationship lasts: "your culture, your background, and...your upbringing" also play a role.

THE ROMANTICS OF THE WORLD BELIEVE IN LOVE
AT FIRST SIGHT. SCIENCE, HOWEVER, SUGGESTS
THAT A NUMBER OF CHEMICALS IN THE BRAIN, AS
WELL AS GENETICS AND BACKGROUND, ALL SHAPE
THE PROCESS OF FALLING IN LOVE AND, PERHAPS
MORE IMPORTANTLY, HOW LONG LOVE LASTS.

100 MYSTERIES

Why Does Sunlight Make Some People Sneeze?

Gesundheit! You step out into bright sunshine after spending a couple of hours in a dark movie theater and immediately experience a sneezing fit. Does this happen to you often? Does it happen to your children?

The Sun induces sneezing in 10 percent of the US population, says Louis J. Ptácek, a neurologist at the Howard Hughes Medical Institute in Maryland and a professor at the University of California at San Francisco. Just how and why this happens, though, has remained a mystery ever since Aristotle raised the question some 2,300 years ago.

Research suggests that the photic sneeze reflex, or PSR, is inherited, but scientists have yet to pinpoint the gene or genes responsible. "There's precious little known about PSR, and part of that is because it's not a disease," Ptácek says. "No one dies from it."

One theory is that the gene involved—whatever it is—crosses wires in the brains of those with PSR. For these people, light entering their eyes activates their brain's visual cortex but also stimulates the motor region that causes the diaphragm to quickly contract, forcing a sharp burst of air out through the nose.

Although Sun-triggered sneezing is more of a quirk than a serious condition, Ptácek says, understanding the science behind it could shed light on the underlying biology of other reflex phenomena, such as certain types of epilepsy.

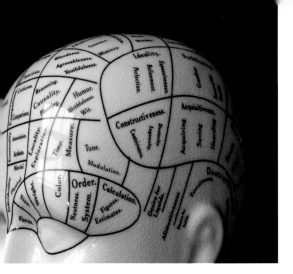

THE QUESTION "WHAT IS CONSCIOUSNESS?" IS REALLY TWO QUESTIONS: WHY ARE WE AWAKE AND AWARE, AND HOW DOES A PHYSICAL NETWORK OF ELECTRICAL IMPULSES GIVE RISE TO OUR SUBJECTIVE EXPERIENCES?

What Is Consciousness?

Perhaps not surprisingly, neither scientist nor philosopher has developed a convincing answer to either question beyond Descartes' "cogito ergo sum" (I think, therefore I am).

In the 1970s, Tulane University biopsychologist Gordon Gallup developed the "mirror test" of self-recognition. If a person or creature recognizes a red dot on his or her forehead in the mirror, the test presumes that the subject is conscious. The mirror test grew out of a modern interpretation of Descartes' maxim that knowledge of self implies consciousness.

Yet it remains unclear why some animals (e.g., humans, primates, dolphins, magpies) pass the test and most others don't. Researchers generally believe that there are specific brain centers that are crucial to awakening and that there is probably something about the complexity of the network of electrical connections in the brain that gives rise to consciousness. How exactly one leads to the other remains a mystery.

Trying to distill the subjective human experience from individual parts of the brain has proven an even more futile undertaking. Adherents of a field called "integrated information theory" argue that some systems are too complex to be understood by breaking them into their constituent parts, and certainly the brain is the most complex biological system known to mankind. This theory gets us closer to understanding why conventional approaches can't explain consciousness, but doesn't go as far as to explain how consciousness should arise out of complex network effects.

With the failure of classical physics to provide an explanation for consciousness, physicists have proposed that the mind may arise via quantum mechanical processes. (Quantum mechanics is the study of relationships between subatomic particles.) Some interpretations of quantum mechanics imply that the world only takes the order it does when observed by a conscious individual. Conversely, the resolution of the random, quantum universe within very small structures in the brain may itself trigger consciousness. However, if these structures do exist, scientists have yet to discover them.

If the search for consciousness seems hopeless at this point, there may be good reason. University of Miami philosopher Colin McGinn believes that the mind is fundamentally incapable of understanding itself. If true, consciousness will forever remain the ultimate scientific mystery.

Can the Food You Eat Affect Your Descendants' Genes?

A recent study suggests that the same vitamins in spinach that perform instant wonders for Popeye's biceps might pack longer-lasting effects, such as dictating the hair color and health of future generations. Your lunch order could make a bigger difference than you think.

A 2006 study led by David Martin, an oncologist at the Children's Hospital Oakland Research Institute in California, tested whether a mouse's diet alone can affect its descendants. The researchers fed meals high in minerals and vitamins—such as B12, which fortifies leafy greens, to pregnant mice that have a gene that makes their fur blond and also increases the likelihood that they will grow obese and develop diabetes and cancer. On the new diet, the mice produced brown-haired offspring that were less vulnerable to disease. Even when the second-generation mice were denied the supplements, their offspring retained the improved health and still grew dark fur coats.

Martin's study isn't the first to note this type of generation-spanning phenomenon. In 2002, Swedish researchers digging through century-old records determined that a man's diet at the onset of puberty affected his grandson's vulnerability to diabetes. The study tracked 303 men, and those with an abundant supply of food were four times as likely to have grandchildren die of diabetes. Though far from exhaustive, the study indicated that genes are more susceptible to outside forces than has been commonly believed.

But don't start your teenager on that all-spinach diet just yet—scientists warn that the influence of diet on human gene expression is not fully understood. Nevertheless, Martin says, "The general implication for human health is an obvious one: An external agent can have an effect for a very long time. Given how long human generations last, the environmental exposures experienced by a pregnant mother can still have an effect 100 years later."

Are Telomeres the Key to Immortality?

Thanks to recent breakthroughs in genetics research, we may be on the verge of discovering a fountain of youth in our own genetic material.

In 2009, three researchers—Elizabeth Blackburn of the University of California, San Francisco, Carol Greider of Johns Hopkins University, and Jack Szostak of Massachusetts General Hospital—won the Nobel Prize in Medicine for their work linking the aging process to telomeres. Telomeres are clusters of DNA that cap the chromosomes of complex organisms, protecting the rest of the genetic code during cell division. As cells age, these caps grow smaller, exposing the DNA to breaks and mutations that can lead to cancer or cell death.

These discoveries hint at a connection between telomeres and the broader aging process. People of an advanced age do tend to have cells with shorter telomeres when that cell is of a type that replicates frequently. Analysis of the white blood cells of Hendrikje van Andel-Schipper, a Dutch woman who lived to the age of 115, revealed extremely short telomeres on such cells compared with cells that divide infrequently (such as nerve cells). Similarly, patients who suffer from accelerated aging diseases have also been shown to possess much shorter telomeres than unaffected individuals of a similar age.

So can we prevent or even reverse aging by preserving our telomeres? Maybe. While early results indicate a correlation between shorter telomeres and aging, this does not by itself imply a causal relationship. It could be that the two processes simply coincide or even that aging itself is what causes telomeres to shrink. And even if the relationship is causal and significant, how do we take advantage of this fact? Gene therapy is still in its infancy. Worse still, telomerase, the enzyme that inhibits the decay of telomeres, is also present in 90 percent of cancerous cells; by preventing cell death, we may grow malignant tumors.

It's worth considering that this relationship serves a purpose. Our genetic code may have evolved to encourage cells to die in order that they might not grow into cancer. If there is indeed a fountain of youth, it may behoove us to blaze a different path on our way there.

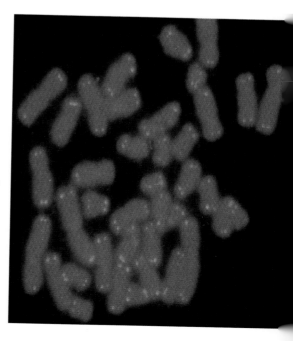

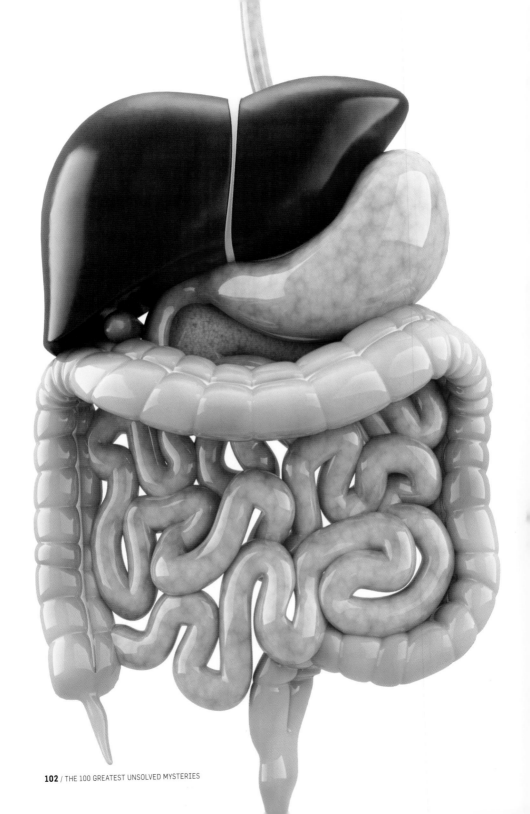

Why Do We Have an Appendix?

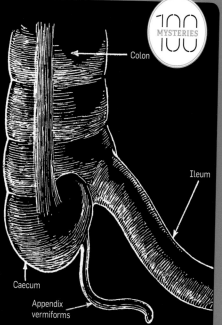

Colon

Ileum

Caecum

Appendix
vermiforms

For decades, scientists have thought that the appendix no longer serves a purpose for the human body. That notion came in part from Charles Darwin. He theorized that the appendix and a section of the small intestine it's attached to, the caecum, once played a role in digestion for our ancestors.

The caecum was where intestinal bacteria used to digest leaves were found. But, according to Darwin's thinking, as humans evolved and began eating more fruit, which was easier to digest, the caecum shrank, and the appendix was no longer necessary.

Recent research, however, suggests the appendix is still important. In 2007, scientists at Duke University Medical Center said circumstantial evidence convinced them that the appendix stores helpful bacteria.

When an infection causing intestinal stress strikes, diarrhea forces most of the good bacteria out of the body along with everything else in the digestive tract. But some of the good bacteria take refuge in the appendix. The tissue there is similar to tissue in the lymphatic system, part of the body's immune system. While the intestinal bacteria hide out in the appendix, the lymphatic system protects them from the illness ravaging the body. When the illness is over, the bacteria go back into the intestinal system to repopulate it with helpful bacteria.

This role for the appendix might be more important in parts of the world where sanitation is suspect and diarrhea common. Duke University Medical Center professor William Parker, who led the 2007 study, says, "In industrialized societies with modern medical care and sanitation practices, the maintenance of a reserve of beneficial bacteria may not be necessary. This is consistent with the observation that removing the appendix in modern societies has no discernible negative effects."

Parker has continued to study the appendix. Among his recent findings, more mammals have an appendix than previously thought (50 out of 361 animals studied, including rabbits, wombats, and opossums), and the appendix has evolved at least 32 times among them. What's still unsure is, if the appendix plays such an important role in preserving health, why don't even more mammals have one?

WE'VE HEARD THAT EVERYONE'S
FINGERPRINTS ARE UNIQUE,
AND WE KNOW THAT LAW
ENFORCEMENT OFFICIALS OFTEN
USE THEM TO TRACK DOWN
CRIMINALS. BUT WHY HUMANS
HAVE THOSE PRINTS IS STILL AN
OPEN QUESTION.

Why Do We Have Fingerprints?

Many scientists once thought fingerprints help us hold onto objects. From an evolutionary perspective, getting a better grip on tools or weapons would have made life easier for early humans. In 2009, Dr. Roland Ennos of Manchester University designed an experiment that tested the gripping power of our fingerprints. He used a machine equipped with weights to pull strips of Perspex, a kind of acrylic, across a subject's fingertips. The machine measured the amount of friction created as the acrylic passed over the tip. In the real world, a high amount of friction between two solid objects in contact with each other would indicate a better grip. In the experiment, the fingertips created some friction on the acrylic, but not as much as Ennos had expected.

Ennos compares our fingerprints to the tires on a race car. Ridges in the tire reduce the surface area of the tire in contact with the road, which reduces friction. The ridges on fingertips have the same effect. Smooth skin has more surface area and so more friction when in contact with an object than fingerprints do. Where fingerprints might provide more grip, Ennos suggested, is when we grab objects with rough surfaces. The ridges on the fingertip extend into the object's depressions and increase the contact area.

At almost the same time Ennos was doing his research, a team of French scientists suggested a possibility for why we have fingerprints. They think fingerprints help gather information about objects we touch and send signals about them to the brain via the nervous system. In their study, the scientists outfitted one artificial hand with grooves on its tips to simulate fingerprints. Another robotic hand had smooth "skin." The hand with the fingerprints was much more sensitive to different surface textures. According to Georges Debrègeas, who helped lead the study, "We believe that fingerprints act like antennas, amplifying the signal."

Other theories about the possible role of fingerprints suggest that they help to divert water and keep our hands dry or that they prevent blisters. To support that second theory, Ennos notes we rarely get blisters on our fingers or the other parts of the body with natural ridges, such as the palms of our hands and the soles of our feet. The ability to pin down what role our fingerprints actually play could help scientists develop more lifelike prosthetic hands.

What Happens When You Die?

Different religions throughout the world claim to understand what happens to us after we die. Scientists are not as certain. They can explain, though, what happens in and to our bodies at the moment of death and just after.

To doctors, clinical death comes when the heart goes into cardiac arrest, which can occur from a variety of causes—from a car accident to illness. In effect, most of us die from cardiac arrest. The heart stops beating, cutting off the flow of blood, and thus oxygen, to the brain. Next comes biological death, as the brain, other organs, and cells stop functioning because of a lack of oxygen.

Before reaching that point, however, in the window between clinical and biological death, doctors have been able to start the heart beating again, thus preventing death, or irreversible brain damage due to lack of oxygen. Thanks to research over the past several decades, doctors can now revive people whose hearts have stopped beating for as long as two hours, without any brain damage.

Sam Parnia, who studies heart resuscitation at the State University of New York at Stony Brook, says doctors now know that some cells, including brain cells, can function without oxygen for longer periods than once thought. After cardiac arrest, Parnia says, people enter a "gray zone, where death can be reversed." The key is chilling the body by about seven degrees as quickly as possible, so doctors can begin the resuscitation process.

Parnia's work has convinced him that even after cardiac arrest has led the brain to shut down, a person's consciousness can remain intact for up to several hours, though, in what Parnia calls a hibernated state. That fact could explain the "near-death experiences" (NDEs) some revived patients report. But beyond those few hours, most researchers believe, consciousness disappears, since, as scientist Richard Dawkins has said, the brain creates consciousness. Without a functioning brain, there can be no consciousness.

Not all scientists, though, share this view. Dr. Robert Lanza believes that quantum physics allows for the possibility that human consciousness is separate from the brain, and that consciousness continues after the body dies. Space and time are not external realities, he argues, but products of our consciousness. The world, in reality, has no space or time, and "death does not exist in a timeless, spaceless world."

Whatever religions teach about life after death, it's clear that science is still trying to solve the mystery of what happens after we die. David Wilde, a British research scientist studying NDEs, said in 2014, "We are still very much in the dark about what happens when you die …"

Is There an Alternative to DNA?

DNA and RNA are the molecular blueprints of life. They encode and pass on genetic information, known as heredity, and they can adapt over time through the process known as evolution. Without heredity and evolution, life would not exist.

Scientists wonder whether these important traits can occur only through DNA or RNA, or if other molecules might be able to perform the exact same tasks.

At the MRC Laboratory of Molecular Biology in Cambridge, England, researchers developed chemical methods to turn DNA and RNA into six alternative genetic polymers called XNAs—xenonucleic acids. The process exchanges the sugar backbone, the deoxyribose and ribose (the "d" and "r" in DNA and RNA), for other molecules. The resulting XNA double helix is more stable than the natural genetic material. One of the XNAs, a molecule called anhydrohexitol nucleic acid, or HNA, is even capable of undergoing directed evolution. So far, the artificial material uses conventional DNA as a foundation, but some scientists hope to make synthetic organisms from scratch someday, creating an evolutionary shortcut.

Artificial XNA will drive research in medicine and biotechnology while shedding light on the original molecules that created life billions of years ago. Alternative DNA can enable scientists to make new forms of life in the laboratory. Medicine may benefit since the human body has not evolved to create enzymes that break down the foreign XNA structure. Perhaps most importantly, XNA proves that two fundamental elements of life, heredity and evolution, are possible using alternative genetic material and that life is not completely reliant on RNA and DNA as previously thought. Some scientists think we may find evidence of XNA in extraterrestrial life. However, if you're worried about researchers creating synthetic life using XNA anytime soon, don't be. John Chaput, a molecular biologist at Arizona State University, says, "That's possible, but much further down the road."

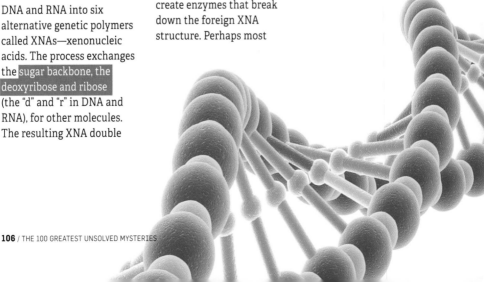

Why Do We Age?

Ponce de León sought the fountain of youth. People today pin their hopes on diets, supplements, exercise, or plastic surgery. It's a fact: Humans age, and lots of us don't like how aging makes us look or feel. But what if we were able to slow the aging process?

Scientists call the process of aging senescence. Why we age, according to Marquette University professor Sandra Hunter, is rather simple: "Cell death…eventually leads to systems malfunctioning and whole body death." For example, muscle fibers and nerves connected to them gradually die, leading to a loss of strength that begins at age 50 and continues steadily thereafter.

A deeper question for scientists is, why do the cells die? They've come up with several theories, and most likely a combination of them explains the aging process. One theory rests on oxidative damage. Normal cell processes release harmful molecules called oxygen free radicals. Substances in the body called antioxidants neutralize some of them, but a few free radicals escape unscathed and damage cells. Oxidative damage is linked to such diseases and conditions as heart disease, diabetes, and Alzheimer's.

Other theories pin cell death on genes, which limit how often the cells can replicate. Parts of our chromosomes, called telomeres, get shorter with each cell division until they are so short the cell can't divide anymore. Like free radicals, shortened telomeres have been linked to a number of illnesses.

Certain genes might also control the life span of an entire organism. Research on worms shows that when scientists mutate genes related to the aging process, they can extend a worm's life to four times its normal life span. If similar genes exist in humans and can be changed the same way, people could live up to 300 years old.

For rats, cutting their calorie intake by 30 percent of what's considered normal lengthens their life span. Scientists predict that similar extreme dieting could have the same effect on humans. And studies in humans have shown that diet and exercise can play a role in lengthening telomeres.

"Metaphysically speaking, we age because time passes without our having died," says Marquette philosophy professor Susan Foster. "Aging, at least, seems to beat the alternative."

When Will We Evolve Out of Our Useless Appendages?

Never. We're probably permanently stuck with our pinky toes, tailbone, and just about all our other evolutionary holdovers. Wisdom teeth could eventually go, but significant changes like losing an appendage (teeth included) take millions and millions of years—who knows if humans will even be around that long? What's more, most of our seemingly useless vestiges are actually helpful.

The coccyx, or tailbone, "is an attachment point of a number of muscles at the pelvis. We need it for upright locomotion. It would be catastrophic if it went away," says Kenneth Saladin, an anatomist and physiologist at Georgia College and State University. Additionally, the pinky toe helps us keep our balance and diffuses impact throughout the foot when we run.

There are only a handful of truly useless parts of our body, but these are hanging on, too. As Saladin puts it, "Since vestiges like the muscles behind our ears have very little impact on reproductive success, there's no way to select against them." In other words, the ability to ear-wiggle doesn't interfere with the ability to have kids.

The silliest of all vestiges is the male nipple. "Those don't have a function," Stearns says, "but they won't disappear, either." All embryos, male and female, begin developing according to the female body plan. Only around the sixth week of gestation do the genes on males' Y chromosomes kick in. "The developmental plan has the two nipples there, so you can't get rid of them genetically, because that would mess up the breasts of females." And nobody wants that.

How Much of the Human Body Is Replaceable?

Fans of the old TV shows *The Six Million Dollar Man* and *The Bionic Woman* saw scientists revive nearly dead human beings, bringing them back to life with high-tech body parts that gave them extraordinary capabilities. Today, replacing parts of the human body using state-of-the-art technology is moving out of the realm of science fiction and into reality.

A lab technician looks at a petri dish containing material populated with liver cells.

Replacement of body parts means transplanting organs and tissues from one person to another or using artificial body parts. Organs currently transplanted are the heart, kidneys, liver, lungs, pancreas, and intestines. Tissues and cells include the corneas, cartilage, muscles, tendons, ligaments, skin, and heart valves (mechanical versions of the valves are also used).

Artificial limbs and organs can replace parts throughout the body. Doctors commonly replace knees and hips, along with finger, elbow, and shoulder joints. Cochlear implants are electronic devices that restore hearing, and researchers are currently testing a new brain implant that can help patients who lack functioning auditory nerves. Prosthetic noses, hands, arms, and legs are available; artificial legs are among the most sophisticated prosthetics today, and researchers continue to improve "bionic" hands with an almost human sense of touch. One, the bebionic3, has 14 different grip patterns, including ones that allow users to pick up a coin or write with a pen.

The science of developing artificial body parts is constantly changing. In 2014, hospitals across the United States tested a "bioartificial" liver that combines liver cells and a mechanical device that together perform liver functions outside the body while a patient's diseased liver regenerates healthy tissue. Researchers in Japan and elsewhere are developing 3-D printers that combine stem cells and artificial materials to custom-make artificial ears. The Japanese team hopes to also create skin and bones using this method.

Scientists are also working to grow real replacement parts in the lab. Doris Taylor of the Texas Heart Institute is one of the pioneers in using stem cells to create such body parts as hearts, livers, and kidneys for transplants. Taylor says, "I absolutely see a day where you'll walk into a manufacturing facility somewhere, and there will be jars of kidneys, jars of livers, and jars of lungs, whatever it is you need."

Why Do Amputees Sense a "Phantom Limb"?

Phantom limb syndrome is the sensation that an amputated limb is still attached to the body and functioning normally.

Amputees report feelings of warmth, coldness, tingling, itchiness, numbness, cramping or tickling in the missing limb. An estimated 80 percent of amputees report phantom pain in their amputated limb, including shooting, piercing, burning, or stabbing pain.

What is the exact cause of phantom limb syndrome? For many years, the favored theory has been that this condition is the result of "maladaptive brain plasticity." In short, when the brain ceases to receive signals from a missing body part, input from another body part, such as the face according to some research, begins to dominate that region of the brain. This "remapping" of the brain has long been thought to cause the syndrome.

Results of a 2013 study conducted by Oxford University neuroscientist Tamar Malkin, however, reveal the opposite. Malkin discovered that victims of phantom pain have stronger rather than weaker brain representations of the missing limb, with no indication of brain remapping. MRI scans of hand amputees and two-handed subjects taken while they were performing other activities, in this case smacking their lips (a testing of the facial region) showed no significant difference in cortex activation in the hand area between the two groups. Malkin concluded that cortical representation of the lips was not taking over areas associated with the missing hand. In addition, lip-smacking movements did not cause pain among the amputees.

"These findings shed new light on the neural correlates of the conscious experience of phantom pain," says Malkin. "We found that the hand area of the brain seems to maintain its originally assigned role, despite the loss of original inputs and outputs," she adds. "Our results may encourage [new] rehabilitation approaches."

Currently, treatment for phantom limb pain includes medication, biofeedback, hypnosis, and vibration therapy. Unraveling the mystery of phantom limb syndrome will enable scientists and physicians to develop better methods of treatment for its symptoms.

100
MYSTERIES

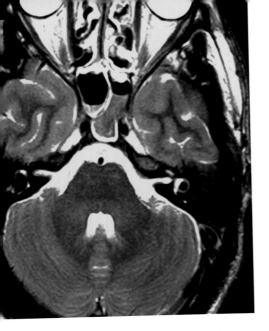

Can You Upload Your Brain to a Computer?

Within the next century, scientists may discover a way of making humans—or at least what goes on inside our brains—live forever.

In a hypothetical process called mind uploading, or mind transfer, all that exists in an individual's brain—memories, personality, consciousness, perceptions—would be transferred from the physical brain to a computational device, such as a computer or an artificial neural network. Theoretically, the brain would be scanned and mapped and its activities transferred to the device, which could then run a simulation of the brain's information-processing abilities. If the process works, the computational device would generally be able to respond in the same way as the original human brain.

In essence, mind uploading means humans could live indefinitely.

Mapping the human brain, however, is no easy task, as neuroscientists working on this technology will attest. The human brain contains roughly 85 billion neurons, each one connected to thousands of others via branches called dendrites and axons. While many people would disagree, some scientists believe who we are—our consciousness, our memories, our personalities—lies solely in the sum of the brain's activity, the patterns of the electrochemical impulses that occur both in our waking and sleeping hours. Researchers

can detect and record electrical brain activity, but they have yet to unlock the mystery of how neurons interact, among other intricate workings of the brain. Many scientists are seeking answers to these stumbling blocks, however, and some predict mind uploading will be a reality one day.

The prospect of such "eternal life" technology has elicited strong responses from opponents. Some claim that the preservation of the brain after biological death would violate their religious beliefs. Others argue that natural aging and death are part of the human experience and it would be wrong to extend life beyond what nature provides. Ethical and legal issues also need to be considered. Political and economic implications would also come into play.

The flip side, of course, is to consider the benefits to humanity of having the brain of an Einstein, a Picasso, or a Lincoln from which to extract knowledge and study. Mind uploading would enable family members to have access to the uplifting and informative memories of long-dead ancestors. In short, the technology holds the potential to enable each of us to remain connected, and contributing, to the society that helped form us.

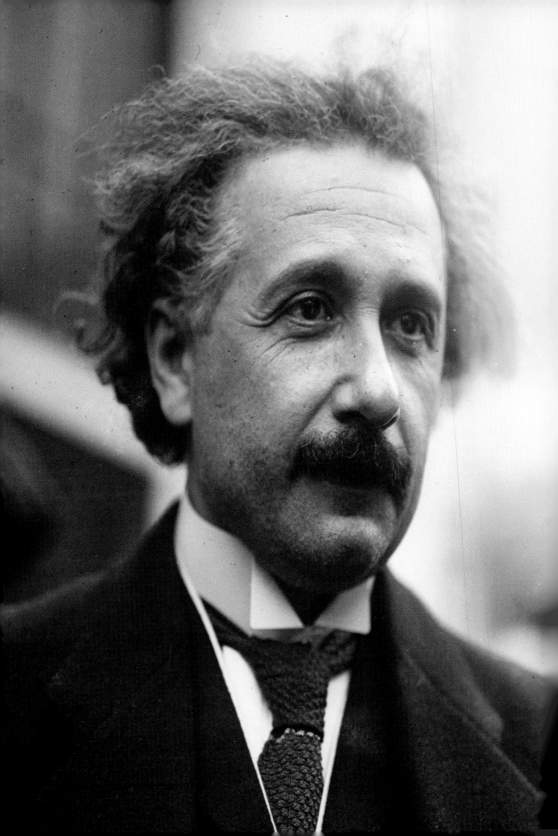

What Is Intelligence?

The true meaning of intelligence is a difficult code to crack. Simply speaking, intelligence is the ability to acquire knowledge and skills. But which skills and how we measure them varies. Furthermore, why do some people, such as Albert Einstein, have superior intelligence?

Academics tend to measure intelligence using intelligence quotient (IQ) tests. French psychologists Alfred Binet and Theodore Simon developed the first modern intelligence test in 1904. Each year, a group of test takers establishes the average intelligence, represented by a score of 100. Since the first tests, each generation seems to have grown in intelligence, a phenomenon called the Flynn effect. When the test subjects retake older IQ tests, they almost always score better than 100. But that doesn't necessarily mean we are more intelligent than our grandparents—we may just be better at taking tests.

Aptitude tests are one way of measuring intelligence, but scholars note that most aptitude tests are biased from the writer's point of view. For example, Isaac Asimov, a novelist and professor of biochemistry, once wrote that he believed himself smarter than his auto-repair mechanic. But if his auto-repair mechanic had devised a test of intelligence, Asimov wrote that he would certainly have failed.

For years, many researchers associated skull size with high intelligence test scores. But in 2007, after decades of research, neuroscientists Rex Jung and Richard Haier published a study describing 37 different neuroimaging studies of IQ. The surprising results suggest that intelligence is related not to brain size or structure, but instead to how efficiently information travels through the brain. The scientists found the frontal and parietal lobes play the most important role in intelligence. These areas also control attention, memory, and language, which Jung and Haier believe is not a coincidence. However, the neuroscientists found that intelligence is scattered throughout the brain; no single region is wholly responsible. Perhaps this explains why some people have higher levels of artistic talent, mathematical skill or musical ability. Since no single structure is responsible for general intelligence, different types of brain designs may produce different types of intelligence.

Understanding the path intelligence takes throughout the brain can boost IQ. It can also help treat people who are intellectually or developmentally disabled. Dissecting how we learn can be an important aid for children in schools. But even an IQ test does not account for all types of brainpower. Einstein himself proclaimed, "The true sign of intelligence is not knowledge, but imagination."

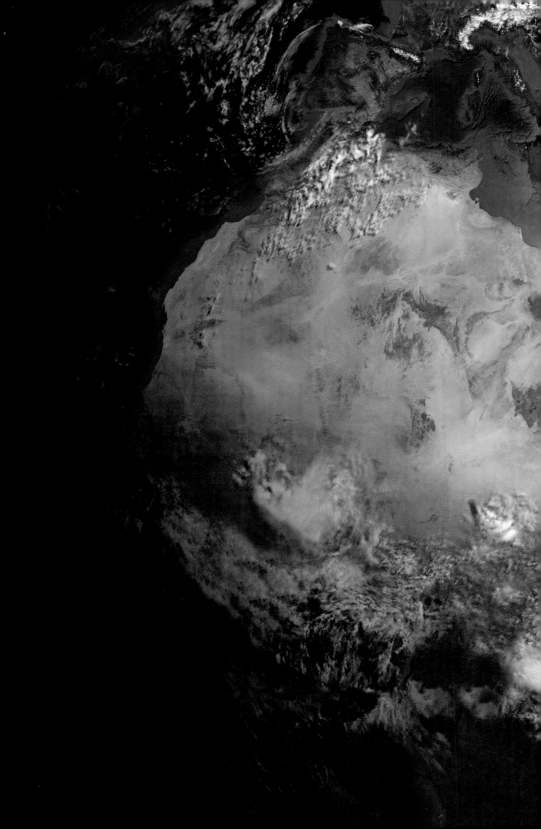

Earth

CHAPTER 4

What Causes Volcanic Lightning?

On March 10, 2010, Eyjafjallajökull volcano, a caldera in Iceland covered by an ice cap, erupted. It sent plumes of clouds across most of Europe and the Atlantic Ocean. Photos of the eruption show lightning originating and ending in the cloud of ash that hovered over the volcanic opening.

The largest volcanic storms are similar to supercell thunderstorms that spread across the American Midwest. But while those thunderstorms are fairly well understood, volcanic lightning still remains mysterious.

The remote location of volcanoes and infrequent eruptions make volcanic lightning difficult to study. In general, lightning occurs through the separation of positively and negatively charged particles. Differences in the aerodynamics of the particles separate the positive and negative, and when the difference in charge is great, electrons flow between the positive and negative regions. A lightning bolt is a natural way of correcting the charge distribution.

So what makes volcanic lightning so difficult to understand? Scientists believe ejections from the volcano into the atmosphere carry a large electrical charge, but they aren't sure if it originates in the volcano or occurs afterward. Very high-frequency radio emissions and other types of electromagnetic waves now allow scientists to observe the lightning inside the ash plume. Since 2006, scientists have used the new technology during three separate eruptions, including Eyjafjallajökull, and can distinguish two phases for volcanic lightning. The first phase, called the eruptive phase, is the intense lightning immediately after the eruption near the crater. Presumably, charged particles from the volcano are the source of this lightning that occurs near the crater. Phase two, called the plume phase, is lightning that forms inside the ash plume downwind of the crater. The origins of this lightning remain a mystery.

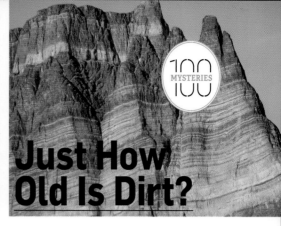

Just How Old Is Dirt?

"It depends on what you mean by dirt," says Milan Pavich, a research geologist with the US Geological Survey. "The oldest sedimentary rocks are about 3.9 billion years old—they're in Greenland—and at one time, they were dirt. That's pretty close to the time the Earth formed."

But those rocks are just proof that dirt existed on the planet way back then. The stuff in your backyard is much fresher. "Most of the dirt you see today is from the past 2 million years," Pavich says. Long ago, the planet underwent major changes that drove the formation of new dirt.

Global cooling and drying enlarged the deserts, and dust storms redistributed that dirt around the globe. Meanwhile, glaciers began extending from near the poles, grinding rocks, soil, plants, and everything else into dirt as they moved over the land.

Dirt is still being produced all the time, albeit in much lesser quantities. Beneath the soil's surface, rocks constantly react with rainwater or groundwater and slowly grind together, breaking down into smaller minerals. So in that respect, dirt really isn't that old. Then again, Pavich notes, a lot of what came out of the Big Bang was essentially dust, which then condensed to form the stars and, later on, planets. "If you think about it," he says, "dirt and its origin are older than the stars."

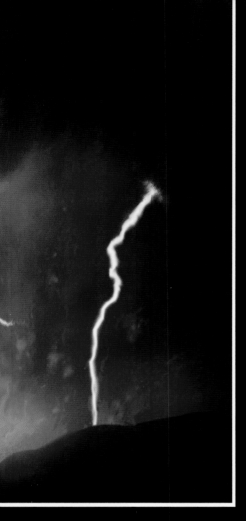

In the 2010 eruption of Eyjafjallajökull, plumes of smoke significantly interrupted airline traffic, resulting in billions of dollars of lost revenue. The more we understand about volcanoes, the better we get at predicting an eruption and the potential consequences. Some scientists hope that studies of the composition of gases inside a volcanic plume could tell us more about the early stages of our planet and the conditions that created the building blocks of life, making volcanic lightning a worthy pursuit. At a safe distance, of course.

How Do Plate Tectonics Work?

If you've ever felt the ground shake beneath your feet or seen pictures of a lava-spewing volcano, you know the effects of plate tectonics.

Earth has three major components. In the center is the core, surrounding that is the mantle, and the outer layer of the planet is the crust. Together, the crust and the top part of the mantle are called the lithosphere, which is about 60 miles (97 km) deep in most places. The lithosphere is made up of eight major tectonic plates and some smaller ones. (The number, size, and shape of plates change throughout Earth's history.) The plates can be oceanic—under the oceans—or continental. Tectonic plates are in constant but very slow motion, propelled by the movement of molten rock beneath the lithosphere.

The location where two plates meet is called a boundary. How the plates interact at a boundary creates different geological and oceanographic processes and activities. Scientists have identified three major types of boundaries. At a divergent boundary, two plates are moving away from each other. Magma fills the gap between the two plates, creating new crust. One divergent boundary is the Mid-Atlantic Ridge. Over hundreds of millions of years, the slow separation of the North Atlantic and Eurasian Plates along that boundary created the Atlantic Ocean.

A convergent boundary occurs where two plates are moving together. At times, one plate might go underneath another, creating what are called subduction zones. The rising of an upper continental plate over a subducting oceanic one creates mountain ranges. Mountains also form when two continental plates meet head on; that's how the Himalayas were created. The two plates continue to grind together, adding to Mount Everest's height. The meeting of two oceanic plates forms deep trenches below the water's surface, as happened in the Pacific Ocean. In general, convergent boundaries produce many earthquakes and lots of volcanic activity.

Sometimes two plates slide horizontally against each other, creating a transform boundary. The area between the two plates can develop transform faults, which can be the scene of major earthquakes. California's San Andreas Fault stirs that state's greatest seismic activity. Los Angeles is on the side of the fault that is slowly moving northward, while most of the state is on the side going south. In a few million years, Los Angeles and San Francisco will lie practically side by side.

The theory of plate tectonics suggests that our planet's landmasses and oceans are constantly changing. Millions of years from now, Earth's surface will look much different than it does today.

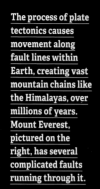

The process of plate tectonics causes movement along fault lines within Earth, creating vast mountain chains like the Himalayas, over millions of years. Mount Everest, pictured on the right, has several complicated faults running through it.

How Big Would a Meteorite Have to Be to Wipe Out All Human Life?

When it comes to meteorites, the bigger they are, the more havoc they generally wreak.

In 1997, University of Colorado geoscientist Brian Toon and colleagues predicted the aftermath of meteorite impacts of various sizes. They found that a space rock a 0.5 mile (0.8 km) wide would produce an explosion with the energy of 100,000 million tons (Mt) of TNT. That's enough to cause widespread blast damage and earthquakes, but nothing too out of line with many natural disasters in the modern age. Once a collision exceeds the 100,000 Mt threshold, you're looking at a catastrophe larger than any in human history. A meteorite 1 mile (1.6 km) in diameter might send enough pulverized rock into the stratosphere to block out sunlight and cause global cooling.

The object that killed off the dinosaurs was probably 7 or 8 miles (11.2 or 12.8 km) wide, says Jay Melosh, a planetary physicist at Purdue University. Its impact would have ejected a dust plume that spread clear around the planet and rained blazing-hot ash onto forests, igniting them. "The dinosaurs probably broiled to death," he says.

Such a collision today would kill billions of people. Those who didn't perish in the initial blast or the fires that followed would face long odds of finding food. "People are going to starve to death," Toon says. Still, a few would likely weather the apocalyptic storm. "Probably some fishermen in Costa Rica," he offers. "People near the oceans who managed to hide out and fish when the fires started."

For a collision to obliterate the human race altogether, Toon estimates it would take a 60-mile- (96.5 km)-wide meteorite. He says, "That would incinerate everybody."

Are We Really Drinking Dinosaur Pee?

You might cringe at this idea the next time you turn on the tap to fill a glass with water, but scientists believe that all water on Earth was at some point consumed and passed by prehistoric creatures. Whether you think of it as water that passed through a dinosaur or water that passed through cavemen, all water on Earth has been recycled.

Charles Fishman, in his book *The Big Thirst*, notes, "No water is being created or destroyed on Earth." This might lead us to believe that we are in fact drinking dinosaur pee, but scientists caution against describing it this way.

The water cycle controls the water on the planet through the processes of evaporation and condensation. The amount of water in the water cycle has stayed the same since the time of the dinosaurs. Nature's ecological filtering process rejuvenates water, continuously breaking down and re-forming the oxygen and hydrogen

bonds. So it's true that the H's and O's are the same since the time of the dinosaurs, but are you drinking the exact water molecules that a *Tyrannosaurus rex* gulped down and later expelled millions of years ago? No, and illustrating the process in terms of dinosaur pee is a negative image that

recycled water can't afford.

Since water resources are scarce in many parts of the world, scientists are experimenting with the idea of turning our waste water into drinking water. Residents in Southern California have been drinking recycled water, endearingly nicknamed "toilet to tap," for decades. While many people can't stomach the idea of guzzling someone else's waste, this form of recycling could be our answer to the water shortage problem. Perhaps if people thought of it as water rejuvenation, there might be more acceptance. The negative perception is driven not by what is in the water, but by the history of where it's been. But ultrapurified water can be certified as much "cleaner" than regular drinking water from the tap. If we can change the negative image, we may soon purchase "Bottled Dinosaur Pee" at the local corner store.

How Do Fire Tornadoes Form?

Veteran firefighters have seen whirling columns of fire shooting into the air. Known as fire tornados, fire devils, fire whirls, or firenados, they can be several hundred feet tall and reach 2,000 degrees Fahrenheit (1,093 degrees Celsius). While most last only a few minutes, which explains why they're not often captured on film, in 2012 an observer in the Australian bush saw several that lasted for more than 40 minutes.

A fire tornado is a vortex—a whirling mass of a liquid or a gas, such as air, that revolves around its own center. A vortex forms when the flows of two forces meet, such as when you pull a plug on a stopped sink. The water rushing downward meets air trying to escape upward through the pipe, creating a swirl of water.

In a large fire, columns of hot air rise. If winds are blowing, the two forces come together and form a vortex. The wind does not have to be intense for a vortex to form. The spinning cylinder of air then picks up burning embers and ash to create a moving column of fire. The firenado can also suck up flammable gases; these and the burning items can spread a fire. Along with spreading fires, firenados can also pick up and toss objects, as tornados do. In 2000, one firenado lifted a small vehicle off the ground and slammed it into an SUV.

Observations by California firefighter Royal Burnett, made in 2008, suggest fire tornados are most likely to occur in desert areas or places experiencing a drought. Those conditions foster the extremely dry fuel, rapid combustion, and high heat associated with fire devils.

According to Andrew Sullivan, an Australian fire researcher, it is difficult to determine exactly when fire tornados will form and how they will behave. Since they usually appear during sudden, strong fires, he says firefighters need to reduce the amount of heat generated as quickly as possible in order to prevent fire devils from forming.

A wildfire in the Great Dismal Swamp National Wildlife Refuge in Suffolk, Virginia, in 2011 ignited a fire tornado.

When Is the Next Ice Age Due?

Ice ages have, in fact, been dominant in Earth's history. Interglacial warm periods, like the current Holocene, are an aberration. Orbital variations and our current warming trend show that the next ice age should begin within the next 1,500 years. Is it time to pack up and move to lower latitudes?

Each transition to an ice age and back is different, because the precise combination of factors does not repeat exactly. This could explain why interglacial periods are not all the same length. Variations in Earth's orbit are one culprit. The subtle wobbles are known as Milankovitch cycles, after the Serbian scientist Milutin Milankovitch, who first described the effect 100 years ago. But the way orbital variation affects Earth's climate is not entirely known. Researchers use data on Earth's orbit to find the historical warm interglacial period that is most similar to our current one. The most recent period, called Marine Isotope Stage 19c, was 780,000 years ago. The transition to the following ice age began with a period of warming and cooling that swung between the Northern and Southern Hemispheres. According to Richard A. Muller at the University of California at Berkeley, the next ice age may occur "any millennium now," but human effects on the environment have altered the trajectory. Even if we halted all current carbon emissions, we will still enjoy a long interglacial period. Atmospheric concentration of CO_2 will probably have to fall below 240 parts per million (ppm) before glaciation could begin. Our current level is about 390 ppm, a consequence of burning coal, oil, and other carbon-rich fossil fuels that release billions of tons of carbon dioxide into the atmosphere.

The Holocene has lasted 10,000 years and allowed the human species to flourish through agriculture, technology, and mobility. "We have taken over control of the mechanisms that determine the climate change," says James A. Hansen, the director of NASA's Goddard Institute of Space Studies. And some think that's not a bad thing, as an ice age may halt food production and could even lead to the extinction of human beings. Groups who oppose restrictions on CO_2 emissions cite the warming trend as a reason not to change our current habits. Scientists agree that humans would be better off in a warmer world filled with greenhouse gases than in a frigid glaciation period. But, they warn, we are not simply maintaining our warm climate but heating it further. Scientists also note the complexity of climate change. In fact, human-induced warming may shut down heated ocean currents that keep the northern latitudes warm, resulting in an even faster descent into an ice age. Luke Skinner at Cambridge University warns, "There are huge consequences if we can't cope with that."

Are Earthquake Lights Real or Illusory?

For centuries, eyewitnesses have reported flashes of strange bright lights in the sky before, during, and after an earthquake. The lights manifest in many different shapes, colors and forms: bluish, flamelike columns rising from the ground; balls of light that seemingly float in the air; and rainbow-colored, flickering flames. The strange phenomena, called "earthquake lights," appear for seconds, minutes, or even hours at a time.

In 1906, witnesses reported blue flames in the foothills west of San Francisco just before the historic earthquake devastated the city. In 1988, a luminous purple-pink orb of light crossed the sky above the St. Lawrence River in Quebec, 11 days before a powerful quake. Seconds before a 2009 earthquake struck L'Aquila, Italy, 4-inch (10 cm) flames of light were seen flickering above a cobblestoned street.

Various hypotheses to explain the formation of earthquake lights have suggested the disruption of Earth's magnetic field in the locale of tectonic plate stress and the piezoelectric effect, in which tectonic movements of quartz-containing material produce voltages that result in flashes of light.

In 2014, a team of scientists led by Robert Thériault, a geologist with the Quebec Ministry of Natural Resources, and Friedemann Freund, professor of physics at San Jose State University and a senior researcher at NASA's Ames Research Center, published a study claiming that earthquake lights appear to embody a different electrical process altogether. The team analyzed 65 earthquakes starting in the 1600s that produced reports of lights. According to Freund, their findings reveal that, "when nature stresses certain rocks, electrical charges are activated, as if you switched on a battery in the Earth's crust." The coarse-grained rocks are basalts and gabbros, which are found in underground vertical structures called dikes, resulting from the cooling of magma deep underground.

When a seismic surge impacts the dike, electrical charges in the rocks are released and funneled upward through cracks in the rocks. "The charges can combine and form a plasma-like state, which can travel at very high velocities and burst out at the surface to make electric discharges in the air," explains Freund.

What Is Ball Lightning?

Imagine yourself taking shelter during a powerful electrical storm. Lightning strikes the earth nearby, close enough for the thunder and the flash to reach your ears and eyes almost simultaneously. You're glad you're safely indoors during such a ferocious storm, but then a startling sight catches your eye: A glowing orb, about the size of a basketball, floats in through the window.

You stare, spellbound, as this orb hovers past, maintaining an eerily steady elevation. Just as you begin to reconcile what you're seeing with your own mental catalog of sights and experiences, the orb explodes with the report of an artillery shell, knocking you to the ground. All that's left is the smell of sulfur and a story your friends will scarcely believe.

You have just witnessed ball lightning.

Ball lightning has baffled and stunned witnesses for centuries. Scientific explanations for the phenomenon ranged from air ionized by cloud-to-ground lightning to vaporized soil, microwaves, and even miniature black holes. One hypothesis held that ball lightning was not real but rather a product of hallucinations. A modern interpretation of the hallucinatory hypothesis proposed that the visions might be caused by magnetic stimulation of the brain resulting from a more typical lightning strike.

Recent laboratory experiments and fortuitous real-world observations suggest that ball lightning is, indeed, a real thing. In 2012, Chinese scientists studying ordinary lightning in northwest China caught ball lightning on a spectrometer. The spectral signature that the researchers captured supports the vaporized soil hypothesis, reflecting the same silicon, iron, and calcium that are found in common soil. Scientists in the lab have also been able to replicate ball lightning by shooting simulated lightning through silicon wafers.

New findings aside, ball lightning remains a science mystery. The vaporized soil hypothesis doesn't explain why ball lightning has been observed traveling through solid objects like windows. Without more data, it remains unclear if ball lightning is a single phenomenon; variations in reports on the size, color, and movement of ball lightning raise the possibility that it could be a collection of several. Nor do these results rule out the possibility that some sightings could be hallucinatory. More experimentation and observations are necessary before we uncover the secrets of this spectacle.

Why Can't We Predict Earthquakes?

Can scientists be imprisoned for not accurately predicting earthquakes? After the devastating earthquake in L'Aquila, Italy, in 2009, seven scientists faced manslaughter charges for not issuing explicit warnings after small tremors shook the area. The seven were convicted, though six later had their verdicts overturned. The original trial judge said the case was not about a failure to predict the quake, but rather about disseminating misleading communication. That's good to know, since no scientist anywhere in the world can predict exactly when or where the next temblor will strike.

Earthquakes occur along the faults between two tectonic plates. While scientists know where these faults are, they never know when the plates will move. Scientists can detect vibrations in the ground right before a major quake, but they don't have enough time to alert people in the area.

Although seismologists can't predict when and where quakes will occur, they can predict the probability of large earthquakes happening along faults. Through the study of patterns of strain in the rocks along a fault, and the history of earthquakes in the region, seismologists can calculate the odds of a temblor of a certain magnitude striking again within a certain time frame. For example, the US Geological Survey predicts that over the next 30 years, the odds of a major quake hitting the San Francisco area are 67 percent.

What about the notion that some animals can sense a quake before it happens? While scientists acknowledge that animals are more sensitive than humans to the first wave of energy a quake creates, we only have evidence that animals detect it seconds before humans feel the more powerful jolt that follows.

Where Did Earth's Water Come From?

Our planet is wet. 71 percent of Earth's surface is covered in water. Most of that water is in the oceans, but another 3.5 percent is in rivers and lakes, locked up in the ice caps, or floating in the atmosphere in the form of water vapor. More fresh and salty water hides beneath the surface, and scientists have even discovered that Earth's mantle is replete with the wet stuff. The watery nature of our home planet makes it unique. So where did all this water come from?

At least some of that water was here at the moment of creation. Scientists estimate that 30–50 percent of the water on Earth today originates from ice from the dust cloud that eventually coalesced into the Sun and its planets. Thanks to Earth's mass, volcanism, and distance from the Sun, our climate now has the right temperature and atmospheric pressure for that ancient ice to exist in a state of liquid water (whereas on other planets, it either froze or outgassed back into space).

But where did the rest come from? For years, the most obvious source was comets—miles-wide snowballs that roam the solar system and could have bombarded the planet in the first billion years. Recent spectrographic observations of comets that buzzed Earth, and the latest findings from the European Space Agency's space probe, Rosetta, point in another direction. The spectrographic signature of the water of these objects indicates higher levels of heavy water—water with deuterium rather than ordinary hydrogen—than is found on Earth. Other findings from Rosetta indicate the presence of a bluish hue on part of one comet known as 67P/Churyumov-Gerasimenko, which would suggest the presence of frozen water beneath the surface of dust and rock. So, if not comets, what and where did our water come from?

The process of elimination leads us to asteroids or, more specifically, a class of meteorites called chondrites, which originated from space rocks in the inner solar system. These potential candidates harbored water on their surface without releasing it, thanks to the younger and cooler Sun, depositing the moisture.

Why Do Earth's Magnetic Poles Flip?

Earth's magnetic poles have flipped many times over the last billion years, switching magnetic north to Antarctica and magnetic south to the Northern Hemisphere. Geologists can see the evidence of reversals in the rock, but clues to how they happened or why are elusive. On average, the magnetic field reverses every 200,000 years. However, the time between reversals varies significantly. The last time the field flipped was 780,000 years ago. So are we headed for a flip anytime soon?

Most scientists believe a theoretical phenomenon, called the geodynamo, sustains Earth's magnetic field. However, aside from somehow drilling 4,000 miles (6,437 km) into Earth's center, there is no way to observe the process. Using a computer model, scientists Gary Glatzmaier and Paul Roberts at the University of California

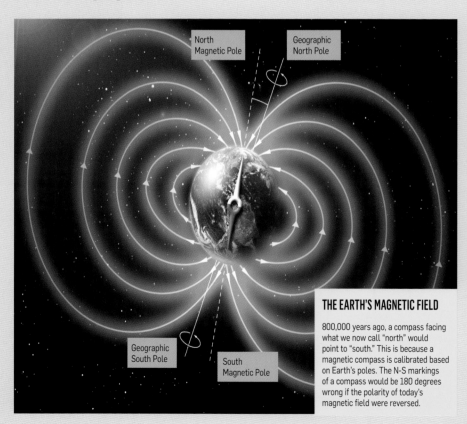

North Magnetic Pole

Geographic North Pole

Geographic South Pole

South Magnetic Pole

THE EARTH'S MAGNETIC FIELD

800,000 years ago, a compass facing what we now call "north" would point to "south." This is because a magnetic compass is calibrated based on Earth's poles. The N-S markings of a compass would be 180 degrees wrong if the polarity of today's magnetic field were reversed.

describe what they believe are the forces that create and maintain the magnetic field. Deep inside the planet, the inner core rotates underneath a liquid outer core made of iron and nickel. The churning acts like convection, which generates electrical currents and, subsequently, a magnetic field. "Once in a while a disturbance will twist the magnetic field in a different direction and induce a little bit of a pole reversal," Glatzmaier told *National Geographic*. These instabilities constantly occur in the fluid flow of the core, tracking like a hurricane through Earth's core, only moving at a snail's pace. Scientists can now pinpoint the boundary where these instabilities in the magnetic field occur. Not long ago, scientists were following a disturbance in the east-central Atlantic Ocean moving toward the Caribbean.

Earth's magnetic field shields most parts of our planet from charged particles in space, mainly from the Sun. Instabilities, like the one moving toward the Caribbean, cause Earth's magnetic field to weaken. Today, it is about 10 percent weaker than when German mathematician Carl Friedrich Gauss first measured it in 1845. Most scientists believe this weakening could lead to a field reversal, but fossil records show it has had no significant effect on living organisms. We may experience more cosmic rays penetrating Earth's atmosphere, and observers might see the aurora borealis at all latitudes. Birds that rely on the magnetic field to fly could become confused. However, as long as the field remains strong enough, the effects should be minimal. And while a geophysicist might say the next big flip is coming "soon," it could still be as many as 10,000 years away.

How Do Icicles Form Underwater?

In the coldest parts of the world's oceans, icicles form on the surface and shoot down toward the ocean floor. They're known as brinicles or sea stalactites, and scientists have only recently detected and begun to understand them.

In the winter, seawater begins to freeze in the extremely cold climates of the Arctic and Antarctic. As ice crystals form, salt in the water is separated from the freezing water. This brine collects in the solid ice in small pools and remains in the ice until it begins to crack. The cracking releases streams of the brine, which is denser and colder than the surrounding seawater. As the brine moves downward, it turns the water around it into a tube of ice that looks something like the stalactites that form on cave ceilings.

In 2011, a camera crew for the British Broadcasting Company filmed the formation of a brinicle for the first time. Some British media called it "the icicle of death," because as it shot downward through the ocean and reached the bottom, it killed tiny sea creatures living there. Smaller sea icicles become feeding spots for other forms of sea life, which eat algae that cling to the brinicles. Andrew Thurber of Oregon State University is one of the few scientists who has seen brinicles form. Working underwater in a dive suit, he examined ones that attract swarming sea life to feed. He compared his experience to "swimming under a beehive. Thankfully, they don't sting."

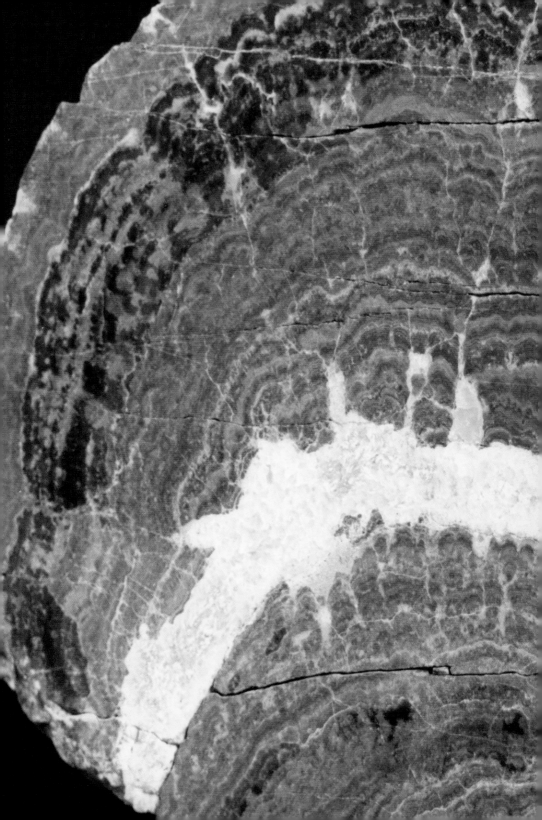

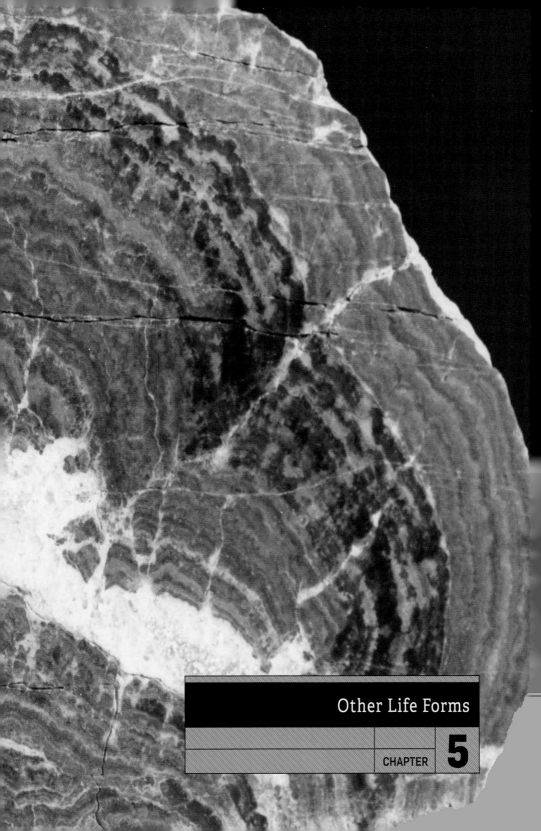

How Did Life Arise on Earth?

RNA

Questions about the origins of life are not only philosophical; many biologists, chemists and geologists struggle to find answers as well. Plants and animals represent just a fraction of the history of life on Earth, which began 3.8 billion years ago.

In fact, for most of the history of life on this planet, microorganisms like bacteria, protozoans, and algae ruled the roost. *Homo sapiens* emerged only 200,000 years ago, accounting for less than 0.004 percent of Earth's history. Most scientists agree that life relies on natural selection and the ability to reproduce, and over the years evolution led us from simple beginnings to humankind. But understanding the origins of life takes some speculation.

Even the most basic living organisms like bacteria are complex compared to the first simple organic molecule that existed on Earth. The long strains of simple nucleotides were a composition of carbon, hydrogen, nitrogen, oxygen, and phosphorus atoms, known as RNA (the precursor to DNA). The living molecules could self-replicate the way

all living things do, while natural selection gave different variants an advantage. Eventually a membrane evolved to surround the genetic material, which proved so advantageous that this type of molecule quickly out-competed its "naked" counterparts. Through natural selection, two-stranded DNA evolved from the simpler RNA into a more stable alternative. This organism similar to modern bacteria became the foundation to life on Earth. Finding proof of where the first organic material came from isn't the hard part. Stanley Miller at the University of Chicago conducted a famous experiment in the early 1950s. Combining methane, ammonia, hydrogen, and water in a beaker (essentially the same components that were present in Earth's early atmosphere), he inserted an electric charge simulating lightning. A few days later he found brown goo in the beaker, which turned out to be amino acids, or the building blocks of proteins. Meanwhile, Harvard biology professor Andrew Knoll wonders about the process of evolution from the simplest of organic material to the complicated living bacteria today. That is, how did life progress from a "warm little pond on primordial Earth that has amino acids, sugars, and fatty acids to something in which nucleic acids are actually directing proteins to make the membranes of the cell?" Somehow all the separate constituents must work together, but scientists are still unsure how that happens. The billions of years between the first sign of life on Earth and today's complex living organisms remain elusive. However, if Miller's experiment is valid, we know that Earth created life, and life changed Earth.

How Do Animals Sense Magnetic Fields?

Capable of returning home from a location more than 1,000 miles (1,609 km) distant, homing (also known as messenger or carrier) pigeons were used to convey diplomatic correspondence, news of great battles, and the results of Olympic contests since the days of Genghis Khan. How did they find their way home? The answer is a sense called "magnetoreception."

Magnetoreception is the ability of organisms to sense magnetic fields. Many biologists believe it is the reason why homing pigeons could so reliably find their way home, why migratory animals can navigate vast distances, and perhaps even why some humans seem to have an innate sense of direction. But how animals can sense magnetic fields remains a mystery.

One hypothesis behind magnetoreception suggests that animals capable of sensing magnetic fields actually possess small amounts of magnetite, a magnetic iron ore, and that perturbations of this internal magnetite help the navigating creature orient itself to magnetic north and south. The discovery of small amounts of magnetite in the beaks of pigeons helps to strengthen this claim.

Another hypothesis proposes that magnetoceptive animals sense the electric induction produced as they move through Earth's magnetic field. Movement of conductive material through a magnetic field induces electricity, so if animals can sense the variations in electrical induction, they may very well be able to orient themselves to Earth's magnetic field.

Perhaps the most promising hypothesis depends on chemical reactions that may take place in the eyes of magnetoceptive creatures. According to this hypothesis, proteins called cryptochromes produce chemical reactions that are essential to circadian rhythms and also to sensing magnetic fields. Proponents of this theory believe that changes in the field affect the chemical reactions that cryptochromes are responsible for, yielding a chemical signal that can be subconsciously interpreted by magnetoceptive creatures.

How Do Animals Migrate?

Navigating is not the same for all species. Short-distance migration is primarily a search for food. Rocky Mountain elk travel a relatively short distance, on average about 15 miles (24 km), to the high alpine tundra in the summer to find lush resources, but retreat to the hills where food is more abundant during the harsh winter months. Along the way they use landmarks, like rivers, to guide them.

Long-distance migration is more complex, determined by the genetic make-up of a species. Arctic terns make the longest migration of any species, from the Arctic to the Antarctic and back—a round-trip of more than 40,000 miles (64,374 km). How they know where to go is mostly a mystery. While birds may be sensitive to the change in latitude, that doesn't explain the accuracy of some migration patterns. Scientists believe birds use Earth's magnetic field, which grows stronger the closer the birds fly to the equator. They time their circadian rhythm to the cycle of the Sun and use the stars to follow a north-south path. Landmarks also provide visual cues. It is probable that birds use several of these methods to calibrate against each other, ensuring they arrive at the same destination year after year.

Protecting stopover areas and winter destinations is key to helping species survive. The endangered loggerhead turtle has seen a resurgence in recent years, due in part to local conservation groups preserving and protecting nesting grounds from North Carolina down to Florida. Since many species travel the same path every year, conservationists are working hard to save important areas that are vital to migration and consequently to the survival of a species.

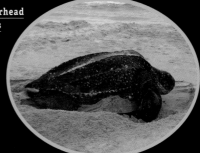

Starting on the southeast coast of the United States, loggerhead sea turtles hatch and begin one of the most epic migrations in the animal kingdom, following the Gulf Stream across to Europe and down the western shore of Africa, then return across the Atlantic Ocean. The solo journey covers an amazing 8,000 miles (12,875 km); the turtles return to the starting point between 6 and 12 years later. The loggerhead turtles take on the difficult migration without an external map or detailed directions. Scientists are still unraveling the mystery of how they find their way.

Why Do Cats Purr?

It's a mystery as old as civilization and as inscrutable as the mighty Sphinx: Why does a cat purr? Despite decades of research, the function of the house cat's purr remains unclear. We know cats tend to purr when we pet them and when they knead (massage soft objects with their paws). Some purr while eating. Some purr while nursing an injury. Some even purr while giving birth. Why would one particular bodily function evolve in response to so many stimuli?

Natural selection implies that unique physiological characteristics evolve to improve an organism's chances for survival. So how does purring improve cats' ability to pass on their genes? Leslie Lyons, assistant professor of veterinary medicine at the University of California at Davis, cites evidence that sonic reverberations at the frequency of a cat's purr—around 20 to 150 hertz—promote bone density and prevent muscle atrophy. House cats use purring as a way to solicit food from their keepers and to signal to their kittens that it's time to feed. In these ways, purring helps cats survive and further their genetic line through their offspring.

However, neither of these theories explains why cats purr in response to both pleasure and duress. Some veterinary researchers, including Lyons, believe that the function of a cat's purr is similar to a human's tendency to smile, hum, sing, or whistle. We might do any of these things when we're happy, but also when we're nervous or unhappy. These behaviors release endorphins—hormones that make us feel pleasure. For cats, purring might release endorphins, either as an involuntary response to feeling pleasure or as a semi-voluntary means of relaxing when stressed.

In addition to the mystery of *why* remains the mystery of *how*. Despite extensive research, scientists and veterinarians have yet to identify a unique organ responsible for producing the purr.

Why Do Ducks Have Orange Feet?

Actually, many species of ducks have feet and legs tinted a bluish green or gray. But for the ducks that do strut around on orange feet—well, it's all about attracting the ladies. Chicks dig orange.

Kevin Ornland is an evolutionary biologist at the University of Maryland at Baltimore County, and he knows as much about mallard-duck coloring patterns as anyone; it was the topic of his graduate thesis. "I looked at male mallards and thought, gosh, they exhibit so many wonderful colors; I wonder which ones females care about," he says. Do lady ducks lust after the males' green head plumage? Or maybe it's the blue patches on the males' wings? Then again, what female duck can resist a nicely proportioned set of white "necktie" feathers? After four years of documenting mallard courtships, Ornland found that none of those features mattered. All the female ducks cared about was the brightness of the guy's yellow-orange bill.

Bright orange coloring suggests that a male duck, also known as a drake, is getting all his vitamins, particularly carotenoids, such as beta-carotene and vitamin A, which are antioxidants that can be beneficial to the immune system. "This indicates that his behaviors and genes are good enough for him to recognize and eat the right food, or that his immune system is strong enough to produce bright orange legs," Ornland says. "The female sees this as a very attractive trait to pass on to her offspring."

Ornland's work only looked at drakes' bills, but he thinks there's enough circumstantial evidence to confirm that ducks check out each other's feet, too. "Blue-footed boobies have, obviously, very blue feet, and it's very well documented that they use their feet in courtship and that females do care about the coloration of males' feet," Ornland says. "Perhaps mallards, like the boobies, have a foot fetish."

Many species are attracted to bright colors in their mate's appearance.

Will Disease Drive Us All to Extinction?

Virulent infectious diseases and parasites have long been shown to be a significant cause of decline in biological populations. But can disease lead to the actual extinction of the host species—such as humankind?

Scientists attempt to determine the extinction-threatening effects of disease by first studying its role in historical extinctions. But proving that infectious disease is responsible for past extinctions is tricky business. After all, the extinct species is not around for scientific investigation. Even if a pathogen or parasite were discovered in a disappearing population, it would not prove that the pathogen itself was responsible for the decline.

However, reasonable evidence exists that historical extinctions and extirpations—local extinctions in which a species ceases to exist in the specific geographic area of study—are at least *partly* attributable to infectious disease. Avian malaria and bird pox are believed to have decimated certain bird populations in Hawaii in the late 19th century. In the mammal kingdom, the abrupt disappearance of native rats on Christmas Island in the Indian Ocean at the turn of the 20th century is believed to have been caused by disease-carrying, flea-ridden black rats that arrived there on a merchant ship.

In recent years, numerous extant species have come under attack by invasive infectious disease. In Australia, koalas are victims to two major pathogens, one of which can cause sterility or blindness. The World Wildlife Fund claims that infections of these types could lead to the extinction of koalas within 50 years. Whether these or other species will disappear remains to be seen, but research indicates that disease caused by pathogens and parasites is not likely to be the *primary* factor in the extinction-threatening process. (Loss of habitat, human overhunting, and competition with new species are possible and/or contributing causes.)

Emerging diseases such as Ebola, HIV/AIDS, SARS, and H1N1 influenza have wreaked

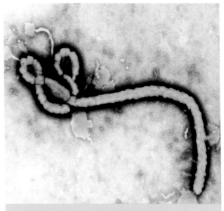

The 2014 Ebola epidemic in West Africa was the largest in history and launched the spread of isolated cases in countries that had never before seen people sickened with the virus.

worldwide societal havoc and resulted in tens of millions of deaths. Reemerging infectious diseases, which appear in new places or in drug-resistant strains, also pose a significant threat to human life. Among these diseases are dengue virus, West Nile virus, and even cholera, which affects 3 to 5 million people each year and causes more than 100,000 deaths annually—despite the existence of a safe and effective vaccine.

What Do Whales Sing About?

Humpback whales sing some of the most beautiful songs in the animal world. It's not just "woo, woo, woo"—their songs last 10 to 15 minutes and have a definite form, usually consisting of five or six unique phrases. Only the males sing, which has led many scientists to theorize that they croon to attract females. The hole in this argument, though, is that no one has ever actually seen a female whale show any interest at all in a male's song.

Male songbirds change their tunes to impress potential mates, but a group of male humpbacks all sing the same song. If the song changes midseason, they all adopt the same change. We don't really know why they sing together. They might be trying to create a sense of peace before they mate, or they could be staking out their territory. Either way, it makes the competitive-mating theory seem less believable.

We're also not quite sure why they change their songs in the first place. It could be that one whale tweaks part of the song, and if it's catchy, the rest pick it up quickly. David Rothenberg, professor of philosophy and music at the New Jersey Institute of Technology, whose book analyzes whale songs, tested this by playing the clarinet to a whale swimming under his boat, and the whale seemed to change his song in response.

Another theory is that whales' brains are programmed to change the tunes no matter where they are in relation to other whales. For example, scientists have made recordings of humpbacks in Hawaii and the Gulf of Mexico altering their songs in similar ways at the same point in the mating season, even though there's no way the groups could be hearing each other's songs.

Most of the research money goes to studying whale songs for conservation efforts (each whale has a unique voice, so it's a good way of estimating how many are out there), not translating their meaning. That hasn't kept the public from enjoying the soulful sounds, however, as several record companies have released albums featuring whale songs. One particular recording by biologist Roger Payne, released in 1970, is the best-selling natural sounds album of all time.

The songs of humpback whales have been instrumental in bringing awareness of their dwindling numbers and the fight for bans on deep-sea whaling.

Can We Clone Extinct Animals?

It's looking more and more likely that scientists will be able to resurrect some lost members of the animal kingdom through cloning. Disappointingly, dinosaurs would not be first on the list—more recently vanished species would offer the most viable DNA samples for reconstruction.

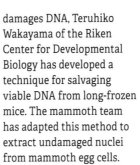

A Japanese team led by Akira Iritani, professor emeritus of Kyoto University, is hoping to deliver a real, live woolly mammoth within five or six years. Mammoths are unusually good candidates for resurrection: Although they've been extinct for thousands of years, their northerly habitat means that numerous mammoth bodies have been found entombed in ice. Although freezing damages DNA, Teruhiko Wakayama of the Riken Center for Developmental Biology has developed a technique for salvaging viable DNA from long-frozen mice. The mammoth team has adapted this method to extract undamaged nuclei from mammoth egg cells.

There's a lot of work still to do, however. The mammoth egg nuclei will need to be implanted in elephant egg cells, and the (hopefully) viable embryo that results would then need to be carried to term by an elephant mother—a process that may well present new problems, despite the strong genetic similarity between mammoths and elephants. But with a little luck and a lot of scientist-hours, we may have our very own baby mammoth to study. And from there, who knows? Pet dinosaurs could be closer than we think.

Could Cockroaches Survive a Nuclear Holocaust?

First of all, nothing would live through the intense heat at ground zero. For instance, the 15-kiloton bomb that exploded over Hiroshima ignited a 1,800-degree Fahrenheit (982-degree Celsius) firestorm that incinerated everything within a radius of 1.25 miles (2 km). Outside that radius, however, roaches, and other insects and smaller organisms, stand a pretty good chance of surviving the subsequent fallout.

The average cockroach can withstand a dose of about 6,400 rads (the standard measurement for radiation exposure). In comparison, the lethal dose for humans is only 500 rads—roughly the equivalent of 42 simultaneous full-body CT scans.

One theory on roaches' resilience credits their weekly larval molt, during which their cells divide half as frequently—and as adults, their cells divide even less often. Because radiation causes the most mutations in DNA that is replicating—which occurs most frequently in dividing cells—this slow replication protects roaches from radiation. So your kitchen's unpaid tenants may indeed be the ones building the next civilization after we check out.

AT THE END OF THE LAST ICE AGE, SOME 10,000 YEARS AGO, SCORES OF SPECIES OF LARGE-BODIED ANIMALS, CALLED MEGAFAUNA, BECAME EXTINCT THROUGHOUT THE WORLD.

What Caused the Extinction of the Megafauna?

Megafauna—any animal weighing more than 100 pounds (45 kg)—once included some of the most bizarre beasts ever to inhabit the Earth: glyptodons, armadillo-like mammals the size of a Volkswagen Beetle; ground sloths weighing 9,000 pounds (4,082 kg) and reaching 20 feet (6 m) in length; megalodons, 50-foot (15 m) sea creatures bigger than the largest great white shark; and beavers that tipped the scales at 200 pounds (90.7 kg). They all thrived for millions of years and then simply vanished.

Some scientists believe that global climate change triggered the mass extinctions, contending that megafauna came into existence in colder, glacial conditions and died out with the commencement of warmer climates. As tundra was replaced with forestlands, species adapted for colder climates, such as mammoths and woolly rhinoceroses, were supplanted by animals better adapted to the new environment, such as deer and pigs.

Illustrations of megafauna that once roamed Earth: a woolly rhinoceros, a glyptodon (an armadillo-like creature) and megalodon, an enormous shark.

human exodus from Africa to new locations across the planet and into these animals' territories was occurring at this time.

Supporters of the climate change theory, however, point to the lack of evidence that human hunters were capable of systematically overkilling megafauna. After all, they reason, one of the world's most widely hunted large animals, the American bison in North America, managed to survive for nearly 10,000 years after it first became a prey for hunters.

Archaeologist K. Kris Hirst offers a more likely scenario for the extinction of megafauna—that combined forces are responsible. Animals that were not able to adapt to Earth's changing, colder temperatures died out. Additionally, colder air may have pushed human populations to migrate, upsetting the predator-prey balance. Easy targets were killed off, or the presence of new pathogens led to extinctions.

As it turns out, the disappearance of numerous megafauna species had negative impacts upon Earth's environment. For example, when gomphotheres, a large elephant-like creature, went extinct in South America about 9,000 years ago, the delicate balance of the region's food chain was devastated. The animals ate in the forest, and their droppings fertilized other areas. "That no longer happens," says Yadvinder Malhi, professor of ecosystem science at Oxford University, "and places like the Amazon are today affected by low nutrition as a result."

Scientists are hopeful that solving the mystery of the megafauna's extinction will help us better understand how other mass extinctions might happen in the future—including our own.

The megafauna, however, had withstood millions of years of environmental change. Why would they disappear simply because the climate warmed? They wouldn't, claim supporters of the human intervention theory: By overhunting, humans were directly involved in exterminating scores of megafauna species. The archaeological record indicates that the

Why Are Bees Disappearing?

Beekeepers first noticed something strange in 2006—unusually large numbers of bee colonies were dying off. Scientists soon called the phenomenon colony collapse disorder (CCD). It was marked by a hive having a live queen bee but few or no adult honeybees.

The loss of millions of bees in just a few years concerned both scientists and farmers. In the United States each year, bees pollinate agricultural crops worth billions of dollars.

Scientists have suggested several theories for the mysterious disappearance of the valued honeybees. These include natural enemies (such as the Varroa mite or pathogens), deficiencies in the bees' diet, farming practices, and pesticides. The pesticides that have received the most attention are a class called neonicotinoids. As the name suggests, they are derived from nicotine, and they were introduced during the 1990s. Once applied to a plant's roots or sprayed on the crop itself, they remain in the plant's system for at least one growing season.

A 2014 study led by Harvard scientist Chensheng Lu found that honeybees exposed to sub-lethal levels of neonicotinoids were more likely to abandon their hive than bees in a control group. The research, Lu's team declared, backed up earlier studies that showed "sub-lethal exposure to neonicotinoids is likely the main culprit for the occurrence of CCD." A US government-funded study, released in 2015, said that the pesticides are probably not the sole source of the disorder, but part of a larger host of causes.

Manufacturers of neonicotinoids argue that the science is unclear about the role their chemicals might play in CCD. After all, unexplained colony losses occurred in the United States before the introduction of the pesticides. And in Great Britain, scientists have found that previous disappearances of wild bees and wasps, also pollinators, occurred at times when farmers changed their practices, such as adding new fertilizers or taking over more wild lands for agriculture.

Whatever the cause, American farmers risk losing some of their crops if colony collapse disorder continues.

Why Do Geese Fly in a V Formation?

In many regions of North America during fall and early winter, you might spot large flocks of geese flying overhead in a large V formation. Typically, one bird maintains the lead position, followed by the others in two lines that fork apart. Why do the geese fly in a V? Why not assume a C or S formation? Recent studies indicate that the V serves two main functions: energy conservation and visual contact.

As a bird flaps its wings in flight, air swirls around its wingtips, creating an upward lift, while air moving off the bottom pushes downward. Flying in a V formation, each goose is generally slightly behind and above the bird ahead of it—a position where the air is getting pushed up. The goose rides the extra lift provided by the bird it is following, thereby conserving the energy required to flap its wings and thus being able to fly farther.

According to researcher Steven Portugal of the Royal Veterinary College in Hatfield, United Kingdom, birds flying in a V formation display unique mechanisms to conserve energy. In a study conducted with northern bald ibises flying in a V formation, Portugal discovered that each bird controlled its flapping strokes so its own wingtips matched the wingtip path of the bird in front of it. In addition, if a bird got too close to or lagged too far behind the first bird, it modified its flapping speed. The apparent objective of these behaviors is to maximize the amount of lift provided by the first bird. "It's amazing how quickly they can respond to any changes [by] the bird in front," says Portugal.

Flying in a V formation also allows geese to maintain visual contact with each other, which helps keep the group intact and flying as a single unit. Military aircraft have patterned their flying formations in the same manner. Researchers study the pros and cons of conserving fuel by reducing drag on the airplane versus the effects of flying directly in another plane's wake.

Human Triumphs and Troubles

CHAPTER **6**

What Was the Purpose of Stonehenge?

On Salisbury Plain in Wiltshire, England, the circle of massive stones known as Stonehenge has been a place of mystery for 5,000 years.

Archaeological evidence shows that the monument was constructed in phases between 3000 and 1500 BCE. The sheer size of the stones is impressive, with some reaching a height of 30 feet (9 m) and weighing 25 tons (22,680 kg). Stonehenge consists of two circles, an outer circle of sandstone from a nearby quarry and an inner horseshoe made of bluestone, named for its blue sheen when wet or cut. Intense speculation surrounds Stonehenge and its original purpose. Many historians suspected the circle of stones was a healing site or temple of worship. Others theorize that it was an astronomical observatory.

One reason Stonehenge remains mysterious is that the site's custodian, English Heritage, a commission dedicated to preserving England's landmarks, does not regularly permit excavations. Most of the data comes from the 1920s, and later the '50s and '60s, but the excavations weren't very well recorded. Some scientists believe that understanding the chronology of when the stones were erected may provide clearer explanations of the significance of Stonehenge.

Recently, two archaeologists gained permission to excavate. Timothy Darvill and Geoff Wainwright think the answer to Stonehenge lies in the bluestones in the center of the circle, whose origins are in the mountains of Wales, more than 150 miles (241 km) away. Wainwright recalls, "The pieces of the puzzle came together when Tim and I looked at each other and said, 'It's got to be about healing.'" They believe that prehistoric people brought the stones from a region with natural springs, which they presumed had healing powers. But how humans moved the bluestones over those 150 miles (241 km) is still unknown. There are no markings left by tools on the stones that would suggest they were quarried from their original location. One theory is that glaciers carried the stones most of the way and humans dragged them to their current spot.

But evidence for this is lacking.

Inducted in 1986 as a World Heritage Site, Stonehenge is vitally significant to understanding life in the Neolithic and Bronze Ages. It is also the most architecturally sophisticated stone circle in the world, spanning more than 2,000 years of continuous use. Today, Stonehenge has a significant role in religion and culture, inspiring paintings, poems, books, music, and films. While thousands of people visit the monument every year, no day is bigger for Stonehenge than the summer solstice when the Sun rises above the heel stone, a rough stone outside the circle. As the architects of Stonehenge likely intended, this helped ancient civilizations mark the passing of time, and serve as a place of ritual and celebration.

About 37,000 people gathered at Stonehenge on June 21, 2014, to witness the event, admiring the longest day of the year just as prehistoric people did thousands of years ago.

How Were the Easter Island Statues Built?

On Easter Sunday 1722, the crew of a Dutch ship sailing in the Pacific Ocean roughly 2,000 miles (3,218 km) off the coast of Chile unexpectedly sighted land. Admiral Jacob Roggeveen was astonished to see the island's coast lined with scores of giant statues. Roggeveen named the island Paasch-Eyland, meaning "Easter Island" in 18th-century Dutch. The current name of the Polynesian island is Rapa Nui.

The builders of the strange stone statues were the descendants of Polynesian voyagers who first settled the island in about 1200 CE Since their discovery, the 887 mysterious carved figures, ranging in height from 4 to 33 feet (1.2–10 m), have baffled scientists and captivated the public's imagination. Large heads featuring broad noses, jutting chins, and deep-set slits for eyes rest on standing or squatting torsos. Expressions on the stone faces are solemn, as if the statues are watching over the land or waiting for something.

The statues, called *moai*, were carved from stone called tuff, an easily workable, compacted volcanic ash. Stone tools were used to create the faces and designs on the statues. Scientists believe that most of the figures were carved in a quarry located in an extinct volcano on the northeastern part of the island. Yet without animals to pull heavy loads or wheels to move stone or wooden platforms, how did the people of Easter Island transport the giant carvings—some of which weigh more than 80 tons—to their resting places, in some cases more than 11 miles (17.7 km) from the quarry?

Some theorists have proposed the statues were dragged across the island, using rope. Others believe the figures were rolled on the trunks of palm trees. Ancient alien proponent Erich von Däniken claims the moai were built and erected by extraterrestrials.

Others offer a completely different explanation. "The experts can say whatever they want," says Suri Tuki, a Rapanui man. "But we know the truth. The statues walked." According to Rapanui religious beliefs, a spiritual force animated the moai. Surprisingly, Tuki's proclamation may actually be the answer scientists have been searching for all these years.

In 2012, Terry Hunt, an archaeologist at the University of Hawaii, and Carl Lipo, an anthropologist at California State University at Long Beach, conducted an experiment in which they "walked" a 5-ton (4,536 kg) replica moai on a dirt road in Hawaii using only ropes and manpower. People holding ropes attached to the forehead of the faux moai stood on opposite sides of the road and rocked the statue forward and back, inching it down the path. A third group of movers positioned behind the moai used a rope to keep the statue leaning a bit forward, without falling.

The team moved the statue 330 feet (100 m) in 40 minutes, suggesting to Lipo that an experienced group of Rapanuians could transport a typical moai from quarry to resting place in about two weeks. The researchers theorized that the builders carved the statues with a curved bottom, to allow an easy rocking motion. The bottom was flattened once the figures arrived at the stone platform, called *ahu*, on which the statues were stood upright.

Not all researchers, however, agree on the "walking" theory, citing Rapa Nui's rugged, hilly terrain. Even the island's roads, they say, were bumpy and uneven. Finally, the statue that the Hunt-Lipo team moved would have been a small-sized moai, leaving doubters to question whether the "walking" method could work for a much larger statue.

What Happened to the Neanderthals?

A quarter of a million years ago, our distant ancestors left Africa and evolved into the ancient humans we know today as Neanderthals. They fanned out across what is now Southern Europe and Central Asia and remained there for 200,000 years.

Yet despite eons at the top of the food chain, the most up-to-date fossil record indicates that *Homo neanderthalensis* went extinct over a relatively short period of time, between 45,000 and 40,000 years ago. Where did they all go?

It seems that our most direct ancestors, *Homo sapiens*, replaced the Neanderthals, but it's not entirely clear why or how. The dominant theory is that *H. sapiens* were simply more fit for their climate and biome thanks to superior evolution. For instance, studies of the craniums of Neanderthals indicate that their brains were better tuned to locomotion and night vision at the expense of higher-level thinking. This would have put them at a distinct disadvantage when it came to hunting in groups, planning ahead, and developing innovations such as using a spear or bow and arrow. Though competitive exclusion can explain the downfall of the Neanderthals, it cannot explain the abruptness of their extinction. Why were the Neanderthals suddenly so uncompetitive after eons of dominating their landscape? Climate change might provide the answer. During the last ice age, slow-moving, large mammals became scarcer in Eurasia. A shift in game populations toward faster-moving, smaller mammals would have advantaged the swifter *Homo sapiens*.

Or perhaps the competition was more violent. Jared Diamond, author of *Guns, Germs and Steel*, hypothesizes a much darker end for the Neanderthals. We know what happens when more technologically advanced civilizations invade the lands of another people: The newcomers slaughter the established population, first with weapons, then through disease. If Neanderthal-era Eurasia were anything like the pre-Columbian Americas, the Neanderthal extinction would have been violent as well as abrupt.

Even while *H. sapiens* were outcompeting their less-advanced cousins, Neanderthals managed to live on—in a way. Recent analysis of the Neanderthal genome indicates there was probably some interbreeding between the two species around 60,000 years ago. While not enough to explain the entire disappearance of the Neanderthals (there isn't enough similarity in our genomes for *Homo sapiens* to have absorbed the entire species), it does mean that we're more like our primitive cousins than we once believed.

Is the Doomsday Argument for Real?

A Swedish philosopher and professor at Oxford, Nick Bostrom has written extensively on the Doomsday Argument. Let's take a look at his explanation.

Consider two contrasting hypotheses: The first, "Doomsday Early," proposes "humankind goes extinct in the next century and the total number of humans that will have existed is, say, 200 billion." The second hypothesis, "Doomsday Late," proposes that "humankind survives the next century and goes on to colonize the galaxy; the total number of humans is, say, 200 trillion."

But how do we know to which end of the continuum—from pessimistic to hopeful—humanity belongs? Using mathematical probability, we might be able to determine an answer if we knew the number of our birth rank, a number that calculates the number of humans who have ever lived and where we are on that continuum—and we have a good idea of this.

Bostrom calculates roughly 60 billion humans have lived on Earth. Based on this figure, probability should help us conclude that we are likely to be a member of the smaller group, 200 billion. From this, we can reason the Doomsday Early hypothesis is *likely* true—that is, given our birth rank, it is highly *unlikely* there will exist 200 trillion humans. "From seemingly trivial premises it [DA] seeks to show that the risk that humankind will go extinct soon has been systematically underestimated," says Bostrom.

The Doomsday Argument has come under intense scrutiny from the scientific and philosophic communities, "yet no one refutation seems to have convinced many people," says Bostrom. It may be unlikely that the Doomsday Argument becomes reality in your lifetime, but if the DA is true, what does it reveal about the future? Scientists urge that we should not simply give up all hope "because we're doomed anyway," but rather make more urgent efforts to reduce threats to human survival, such as nuclear war, disease, and global warming. Humanity's life expectancy could also increase if humans evolved into a more advanced species, something "other" than human beings, but that assumes we have enough time left to develop the technology to make that happen. It is also possible that the population of Earth declines in the next century, which would change our birth rank. The elements of the Doomsday Argument remain fluid, but the compelling nature of the argument makes it such that study will continue on it in the years to come.

THE DOOMSDAY ARGUMENT (DA) UTILIZES PROBABILITY REASONING TO PREDICT HUMANKIND'S PROSPECTS FOR SURVIVAL.

Why Can't the Voynich Manuscript Be Deciphered?

Polish antique book collector Wilfrid Voynich was convinced he hit the jackpot when he purchased a highly unusual manuscript in Italy in 1912. It was written in a strange script and profusely illustrated with images of plants, the cosmos and zodiac, and naked women cavorting in bathing scenes. Voynich himself acknowledged the difficult task that lay ahead: "The text must be unraveled and the history of the manuscript must be traced."

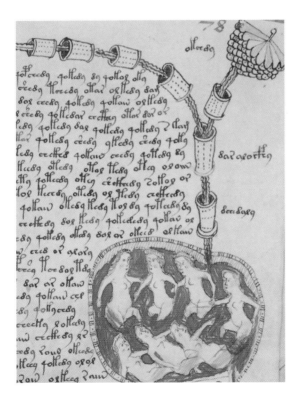

The Voynich manuscript is a codex written on vellum sheets, measuring 9.25 inches (23.5 cm) by 4.5 inches (11.2 cm). The codex is composed of roughly 240 pages, with a blank cover that does not indicate a title or author. The text consists of "words" written in an unknown "alphabet" and arranged in short paragraphs. Many researchers say the work seems to be a scientific treatise from the Middle Ages, possibly created in Italy. The time frame, at least, seems correct: In 2009, the Voynich manuscript was carbon-dated to 1404–1438.

There's only one problem: The contents of the book are a complete mystery—and not a single word of it can be understood.

The enigma of the manuscript certainly isn't due to a lack of research and careful study. The text had already been analyzed for many decades before Voynich purchased it. Once in possession of the codex, Voynich embarked on a brisk campaign to have its text deciphered, supplying photocopies to several experts. Since then, dozens of cryptographers and linguists have tried and failed to crack the code and decipher its base language. Astronomers, historians, chemists, mathematicians, and scores of laypeople have also proposed solutions, but none has shed any light on what the text *says*. Botanists, however, have identified many of the plant species as New World or European.

Indeed, the Voynich manuscript may actually contain no meaningful content, possibly because it was a deliberate deception on the part of its author or because its meaning became muddled in the writing process. In 2007, Austrian mathematician Andreas Schinner claimed the manuscript may have been created by "an autistic monk, who subconsciously followed a strange mathematical algorithm in his head."

To this day, scholarship, speculation, and debate over the meaning of the Voynich manuscript continue unabated. Among recent theories are that the manuscript was written by a young Leonardo da Vinci or by Cornelius Drebbel, a 17th-century chemist and optics developer, in collaboration with English philosopher Francis Bacon, which would put the carbon dating calculations into question. Another theory suggests the document originated with the Aztecs in Central America.

And of course, there *is* the possibility that the manuscript is a hoax.

Is the Antikythera Mechanism the World's First Analog Computer?

In 1901, divers exploring the remains of an ancient shipwreck off the Greek island of Antikythera, northwest of Crete, recovered a bizarre-looking mechanical object that baffled the international scientific community.

The mysterious device, found in 82 fragments heavily encrusted with corrosion, is composed of 30 bronze gear wheels covered with Greek inscriptions. Decades of scientific examination revealed that the ancient device, called the Antikythera mechanism, is an analog computer—the world's first—designed to calculate the position of heavenly bodies, predict eclipses, and even pinpoint the dates of the Olympic Games.

In 2014, James Evans, professor of physics at the University of Puget Sound, and Christián Carman, history of science professor at the University of Quilmes, Argentina, published an article in the *Archive for History of Exact Science* claiming that the mechanism was timed to begin in 205 BCE, establishing the device to be as many as 100 years older than most researchers thought. The incredibly complex machine was engineered and built by ancient Greeks, although "it's probably safer not to try to hang it on any one particular

famous person," according to Evans. The researchers believe the mechanism was designed on Babylonian arithmetic principles adopted by the Greeks.

The front dial of the mechanism features two concentric scales that represent the movement of the twelve zodiac constellations in the sky. The outer ring is marked with the months of the 365-day Egyptian calendar in Greek letters, while the inner ring is marked with the Greek symbols of the zodiac. The rear face of the mechanism includes numerous dials believed to predict lunar and solar eclipses. The mechanism was operated by turning a small crank that was linked to the largest gear on the front dial.

In 2012, in an exhaustive study of the Antikythera mechanism, researchers Tony Freeth and Alexander Jones concluded that the device is "the sole witness to a lost history of brilliant engineering, a conception of pure genius, one of the great wonders of the ancient world—but it didn't really work very well!" The researchers attributed the mechanism's lack of exactness to its imprecise mechanical engineering and the inaccurate mathematical and celestial theories of the time.

To date, no other ancient machine like the Antikythera mechanism has been found. The story behind this ancient marvel of engineering has been long lost to time.

What Caused the Decline of the Mayan Civilization?

The collapse of the Mayan civilization at the end of the so-called classic period, between 200 and 900 CE, is a persistent archaeological mystery.

The classical Maya were the most advanced of the pre-Columbian civilizations, anchored by a collection of city-states in the lowlands of modern-day Guatemala, Belize, and the Yucatan Peninsula. But around 700, these city-states began an inexorable decline that ended in their total abandonment. While the independent Maya survived until the Spanish conquest in the late 17th century, the postclassical Maya were a less urban and populous civilization.

Archaeologists have posited a number of theories explaining the decline of the classical Maya, from foreign invasion to disease epidemic to a collapse in trade with neighboring cultures, but one of the oldest and most persistent theories centers on drought. The Yucatan Peninsula and Petén Basin were already particularly susceptible to variability in rainfall—the soil is thin and sandy, and a regular seasonal drought complicates agricultural productivity. Though the Maya had solved this problem through advances in fertilization and irrigation, studies of soil and stalagmites in the region indicate a decline in rainfall of between 25 and 40 percent in the late classical period. For a culture living off an already fickle water supply, this megadrought may have been too much for even advanced Mayan hydrological engineering to overcome.

Drought by itself, however, doesn't explain the fall in its entirety. It doesn't explain why the Maya didn't return to the classical cities after the climate righted itself in the second millennium or why the northern cities that ascended in the aftermath never reached the heights of the lowland city-states. Nor is it clear why the drought occurred in the first place. It may have been cyclical, but some researchers believe that the Maya instigated the drought by clear-cutting rain forest, cutting short the water cycle that topped off the reservoirs that slaked their thirst during the dry periods.

Almost as mysterious as the decline of the Maya is the fact that the classic Mayan civilization took root where it did. Dense, urban settlements dependent on agriculture have not historically thrived in jungle climates rooted in limestone soil. That the Maya flourished there at all is testament to the ingenuity of their civilization.

How Were the Pyramids Built?

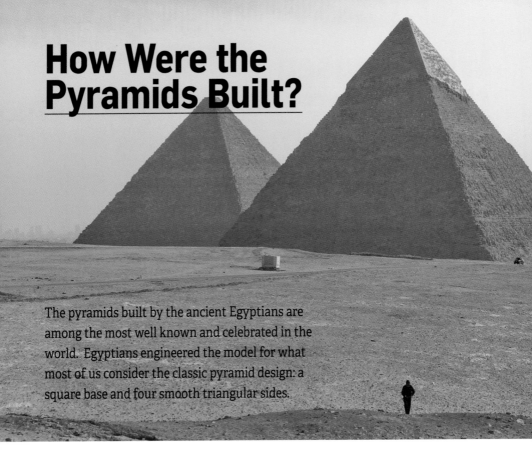

The pyramids built by the ancient Egyptians are among the most well known and celebrated in the world. Egyptians engineered the model for what most of us consider the classic pyramid design: a square base and four smooth triangular sides.

The awesome design and massive size of the pyramids have evoked some fanciful explanations. Some people have suggested that inhabitants of the legendary Atlantis civilization, the biblical Noah, and even extraterrestrials built them, while others claim levitation was used or that the Egyptians possessed a now-lost, unique technology to help them erect the remarkable structures.

Indeed, there is no known Egyptian hieroglyph or relief or any surviving written account from that time depicting the building of the pyramids. For centuries, Egyptologists, scientists, engineers, writers, and mathematicians have theorized how the pyramids were built. All agree, however, about the basic techniques of pyramid construction.

Copper chisels were used to quarry soft rocks such as sandstone and limestone, while dolerite, a hard, black igneous rock, was used on granite and diorite. The blocks were transported from quarries usually located in Aswan to the construction sites down the Nile River on rafts or barges during the rainy season.

Without knowledge of the wheel, pyramid builders used teams of oxen or manpower to drag the stones—many weighing more than 60 tons (54 metric tons)—on a smoothed, level surface built from the Nile to the construction site. The stones were pulled on sleds or on rolling logs, and the roadways may have been lubricated with oil or water.

The big debate of archaeologists, scientists, and professionals centers upon exactly how the massive stone blocks were lifted to the top of the pyramid as it was

constructed upward. Extant ramps—made of mud, brick, earth, or rubble mixed with fragments of brick for added stability and strength—have been found at several pyramid sites over the years. Some Egyptologists theorize that side ramps could have been erected, spiraling around the four sides of the structure, while others suggest a steep staircase-type ramp. Some propose a straight, sloping ramp built from the ground to each side, which was constantly raised as the pyramid rose. One recent theory suggests that two types of ramps were used: an external ramp to build the bottom portion of the pyramid and an internal ramp to complete the structure.

Recently discovered tombs of pyramid workers indicate that the structures were built by paid laborers, rather than by slaves as previously believed. Many of the laborers were farmers and local villagers, who may have considered it a high honor to work for the pharoahs (who were thought to be divine) and build their monuments. The workers were provided food, clothing, and decent housing, and many received tax breaks and other perks for their efforts. Modern Egyptologists estimate as many as 30,000 laborers worked on a single pyramid.

Whatever the exact construction process, it is undeniable that the ancient Egyptians engineered some of humankind's most massive and awe-inspiring building projects. Archaeologists are certain that they achieved their success without supernatural aid—and certainly without the assistance of alien beings.

Glossary

absolute zero The theoretical temperature 0° Kelvin (-273.15°C or -459.67°F) at which no heat exists and particle motion ceases.

asteroid A body of rock orbiting a solar system's sun, occasionally forming belts.

atom The basic and smallest unit of matter and of a chemical element.

big bang The current theory among cosmologists in which matter expanded from a hot, dense point and created the universe.

biochemistry The scientific study of chemical/physiochemical functions in living organisms.

caldera A large depression formed in a volcano, either by eruption of by the surface collapsing in to a chamber/reservoir that once held magma.

cisgender Of, relating to, or being a person whose gender identity corresponds with the sex the person had or was identified as having at birth.

Colony Collapse Disorder (CCD) The state of a colony of bees when worker bees disappear on a large scale while a queen and food, nurse bees, and young bees remain.

consciousness A state of awareness of itself and its surroundings in the mind of a living organism.

cosmologist A scientist who studies astronomy, physics, and astrophysics in regards to the physical origins and evolutions of the Universe, as well as its nature on a large scale.

Doomsday Argument A theory predicting the future population of the human race based off the number of humans born already.

Ebbinghaus Illusion An optical illusion named for German psychologist Hermann Ebbinghaus in which multiple objects are perceived differently, or, relative to their actual size and perception.

electromagnetic spectrum The full range of wavelengths and frequencies of electromagnetic radiation.

extraterrestrial Any object or being from, originating, or existing beyond the Earth and its atmosphere. The term is often used to reference alien life, but also describes non-living bodies and objects in space.

fossil fuels Fuels formed naturally from remains of long-dead organisms such as coal and gas.

Goldilocks Zone The zone, in relation to temperature near a star such as the Sun, where liquid water can exist on a planet. The name is a reference to the children's story "Goldilocks and the Three Bears."

Homo sapien The scientific name for the only human species to survive descended from genus Homo.

hydrocarbons Organic compounds containing only carbon and hydrogen and often occurring in petroleum, natural gas, coal, and bitumens.

Integrated Information Theory A theory that attempts to explain the phenomenon of consciousness and if or why it could be related to physical functions.

magnetoreception A trait in an organism, including some animals, to perceive magnetic fields. This perception allows for senses of direction, altitude, and location.

meteorite A meteor, or fraction of a meteor, that has landed on Earth after surviving the journey through its atmosphere. Meteorites are commonly made of rock with some partially made of iron and nickel.

Neanderthals A previous species of the Homo genus, *Homo neanderthalensis*, that went extinct. Neanderthals are the closest historical relatives to *Homo sapiens*.

neurons Cells that transmit nerve impulses, 100 billion of which reside in the human brain.

neuroscience The scientific study of the human nervous system.

protons A subatomic particle in every atom's nucleus with an equal, opposite charge to the electron.

protozoa Single-celled organisms that live in water or as parasites, such as amoebas, flagellates, and ciliates.

singularity A point or region of infinite mass density at which space and time are infinitely distorted by gravitational forces and which is held to be the final state of matter falling into a black hole.

The Wick Effect The phenomenon that refers to the partial destruction of a human body when burned by fire, specifically, when the clothing absorbs melted human fat.

X-ray A type of electromagnetic radiation often used for taking images, such as those of human bones.

Further Information

Brown, Greg, and Mitchell Moffit. *AsapSCIENCE: Answers to the World's Weirdest Questions, Most Persistent Rumors, and Unexplained Phenomena.* New York, NY: Scribner, 2015.

Gott, Richard J., Michael A. Strauss, and Neil deGrasse Tyson. *Welcome to the Universe: An Astrophysical Tour.* Princeton, NJ: Princeton University Press, 2016.

Green, Dan. *The Science Book* (Big Ideas Simply Explained). New York, NY: DK Publishing, 2014.

Grinspoon, David. *Earth in Human Hands: Shaping Our Planet's Future.* New York, NY: Grand Central Publishing, 2016.

Ingram, Jay. *The Science of Why: Answers to Questions About the World Around Us.* Toronto, ON: Simon and Schuster Canada, 2016.

Kirschvink, Joe, and Peter Ward. *A New History of Life: The Radical New Discoveries About the Origins and Evolution of Life on Earth.* New York, NY: Bloomsbury Press, 2015.

Kleinman, Daniel Lee, and Sainath Suryanarayanan. *Vanishing Bees: Science, Politics, and Honeybee Health.* (Nature, Society, and Culture.) New Brunswick, NJ: Rutgers University Press, 2016.

Krauss, Lawrence M. *The Greatest Story Ever Told–So Far: Why Are We Here?* New York, NY: Atria, 2017.

Mushlin, Stuart B. *Playing the Ponies and Other Medical Mysteries Solved.* New Brunswick, NJ: Rutgers University Press, 2017.

Osman, Jheni. *The World's Great Wonders: How They Were Made & Why They Are Amazing.* Oakland, CA: Lonely Planet Publications, 2014.

Websites

The 7 Biggest Mysteries of the Human Body
https://www.livescience.com/34095-biggest-mysteries-human-body.html
This article explores some of the characteristics of the human body that have not yet been explained by science.

NASA
https://www.nasa.gov
NASA's website offers information on a wide range of topics related to space exploration, including articles on technology, the solar system, and space missions. The website also features images and videos of space, as well as lesson plans and activities for educators and students.

Physics News
https://phys.org/physics-news/
This website provides an archive of articles on the latest discoveries and innovations in the field of physics.

Index

A

aboriginal Australians, 13
adrenaline, 72, 96
aging, 108
Aguirre, Anthony, 51
Akira Iritani, 144
Alexander, Stephon, 15
alien life, 30
Allamandola, Louis, 36
allergies, peanut, 75
alternative universes, 50–51
amygdala, 84
Andel-Schipper, Hendrikje van, 101
Anderson, Adam, 86
anhydrohexitol nucleic acid (HNA), 106
animals
  extinct, cloning, 144
  migration of, 138
  sensing of magnetic fields by, 137
Antikythera mechanism, 164
antioxidants, 108
appendix (internal organ), 103
aptitude tests, 114–115
Arctic terns, migration of, 138
Aristotle, 14
artificial limbs, 110–111
Asimov, Isaac, 115
asteroids, deflection of, 48
atoms, 18
aurora borealis, 64–65
Australians, aboriginal, 13
avian malaria, 141

B

Bacon, Francis, 14, 163
bacteria
  appendix and, 103
  on Mars, 30
ball lightning, 129
Barrett, Deirdre, 79
baryonic matter, 55
bees, disappearance of, 148–149
Bell Burnell, Jocelyn, 29
BICEP2 telescope, 50, 51

Big Bang, 44, 51, 50–51
Big Crunch, 44, 46, 47
Big Freeze, 45, 46
Big Rip, 45, 46, 47
Binet, Alfred, 115
bird pox, 141
birds, v-formation flight of, 150–151
Black, Donald, 73
black holes
  bottom of, 34–35
  star explosions and, 62
Blackburn, Elizabeth, 101
blushing, 72
boomerangs, 12–13
Borge, Victor, 80
Bostrom, Nick, 160
brain
  consciousness and, 99
  déjà vu and, 88–89
  dreaming and, 78–79
  emotion and, 86
  intelligence and, 114–115
  laughter and, 80–81
  love and, 96–97
  memory and, 76–77
  of men and women, compared, 91
  percentage used, 87
  plasticity of, 92, 111
  sleeping and, 92–93
  sneezing and, 98
  uploading to computer, 112
  workings of, 84–85
B612 Foundation, 48
"bubble fusion" reaction, 16
Burnett, Royal, 124

C

calorie intake, 108
carbon atoms, 18
Carman, Christián, 164
carrier pigeons, 137
Cash, Webster, 31
Cassini spacecraft, 67
cats, purring of, 139
cellphone theory, 89
cells
  death of, 108
  longevity and, 101
  noise from, 82–83
cerebellum, 84
Chaput, John, 106

chondrites, 131
chromosomes, 90
cloning extinct animals, 144
coccyx, 109
cochlear implants, 110
cockroaches, 145
cold fusion, 16–17
cold water, freezing of, 14
combustion, human, 22–23
computer, uploading brain to, 112
condensation, 123
consciousness, 99, 105
convergent boundaries, 120
core of Earth, 120
Cowley, Steve, 20
Crab Nebula, 28–29
crust of Earth, 120
cryptochromes, 137
Curiosity rover, 30

D

Däniken, Erich von, 157
dark energy
  end of universe and, 44–45
  general explanation of, 42–43
  shape of universe and, 46–47
dark matter, 54–55
Dark Sector Lab (DSL), 50
Darvill, Timothy, 154
Darwin, Charles, 72, 103
Dawkins, Richard, 105
death, 105
Debrègeas, Georges, 104
déjà vu, 88–89
de Jong, Peter, 72
deoxyribonucleic acid. See DNA (deoxyribonucleic acid)
Descartes, René, 14, 99
Diamond, Jared, 159
dieting, 108
diffraction, 10
dinosaurs
  destruction of, 122
  water and, 123
dirt, age of, 119
disc galaxies, 49
disease, 141

dissolved gases, 14
Ditzen, Beate, 96
divided attention, 89
DNA (deoxyribonucleic acid).
   See also genes
   alternative to, 106
   cloning extinct animals using,
      144
   longevity and, 101
   origin of life and, 136
Doomsday Argument, 160–161
dopamine, 96
Doppler Effect, 10
dreaming, 78–79
Drebbel, Cornelius, 163
DTI scan, 91
ducks, color of feet of, 140

E

Earth
   core of, 120
   life on, origin of, 136
   life on, supernova's effect on, 68–69
   magnetic poles on, flipping of,
      132
   water on, origin of, 131
earthquakes
   inability to predict, 130
   light flashes before, 128
Easter Island statues, 156–157
Ebbinghaus illusion, 33
Egyptian pyramids, 166–167
Einstein, Albert, 10–11
   black holes and, 34, 35
   empty space concept and, 42
   general relativity theory of, 35,
      46, 60
   gravity and, 60
   special relativity theory of, 19
elevator to space, 58–59
Eliot, T.S., 45
elk, migration of, 138
embarrassment, 72
emotion, 86
empty space, 42
end of universe, 44–45
energy, dark. See dark energy
Energy Catalyser (E-Cat), 16
Ennos, Roland, 104
Esser, John "Ernie," 12

Evans, James, 164
evaporation, 14, 123
event horizon, 35
Everett, Hugh, 51
expansion of universe, 44–45
extinction
   cloning extinct animals, 144
   of humankind, 90, 141, 160–161
   of megafauna, 146–147
   of Neanderthals, 158–159
extraterrestrial life, 30
Eyjafjallajökull volcano, 118

F

Faherty, Michael, 22
faster-than-light travel (FLT), 19
feelings, 86
Fermi bubbles, 26–27
fingerprints, 104
fire tornadoes, 124
Fischer, John, 22
Fisher, Helen, 96
Fishman, Charles, 123
Fleischmann, Martin, 16
Flynn effect, 114
food, effects on descendants'
   genes, 100
Fornax constellation, 44
Foster, Susan, 108
free radicals, 108
Freeth, Tony, 164
freezing of water, 14
Freud, Sigmund, 78
Freund, Friedemann, 128
friction, fingerprints and, 104
frontal lobe, of brain, 84, 115
frost, 14
Frost, Robert, 45
fur, lack of on humans, 95
fusion
   cold, 16–17
   nuclear, 20–21

G

Gallup, Andrew, 74
gamma rays
   causes of bursts from, 56–57
   destruction of life by, 68, 69
   Fermi bubbles and, 27
Gardner, Peter, 83

gases, dissolved, 14
Gauss, Carl Friedrich, 133
Geary, David, 91
geese, v-formation flight of, 150–151
general relativity, theory of, 35, 46, 60
genes
   and cell death, 108
   and food's effect on
      descendants, 100
geodynamo, 132
Gimzewski, Jim, 82
Glatzmaier, Gary, 132
global warming, 127
glyptodons, 146, 147
Goldilocks Zone, 40
gomphotheres, 147
Graves, Jenny A. Marshall, 90
gravitons, 61
gravity, 60–61
   dark matter and, 55
   on Mars, 52
   shape of universe and, 46–47
Great Red spot, on Jupiter, 39
greenhouse gases, 127
Greider, Carol, 101
gyroscopic precession, 12

H

habitable planets, 40–41
Haier, Richard, 115
hallucinations, 129
Hansen, James A., 127
Harris, Judith Rich, 95
Hawking, Stephen, 30, 35
Hess, Christian, 74
Hewish, Antony, 29
hiccuping, 94
hippocampus, 84
Hirst, K. Kris, 147
Hobson, Allan, 78
Holocene period, 127
holodecks, 66
hologram theory, 89
Homo neanderthalensis, 158–159
hormones, love and, 96
hot water, freezing of, 14
hottest temperature, 15
Hubble, Edwin, 42, 44
Hughes, Jennifer, 90
human body. *See also* brain; DNA

aging, 108
appendages, "useless," 109
appendix, purpose of, 103
blushing, 72
cells, noise from, 82–83
death, 105
déjà vu, 88–89
dreaming, 78–79
emotion, 86
fingerprints, 104
food's effects on descendants' genes, 100
fur lacking on, 95
hiccuping, 94
laughter, 80–81
longevity, 101
memory, 76–77
parts of, replacement of, 110
peanut allergies, 75
sleeping, 92–93
sneezing from sunlight, 98
tickling, 73
Y chromosome, 90
yawning, 74
human combustion, spontaneous, 22–23
humpback whales, 142–143
Hunt, Terry, 157
Hunter, Sandra, 108
Huygens, Christiaan, 10
hypernovas, 57

I

ice age, next, 127
icicles, formation under water, 133
IllumiRoom, 66
immune system, 75, 103
inflation theory, 51
integrated information theory, 99
intelligence, 114–115
International Asteroid Warning Network, 48
International Thermonuclear Experimental Reaction (ITER), 20
Interpretation of Dreams, The (Freud), 78
IQ tests, 114–115

J

Jeng, Monwhea, 14

Jimenez, Raul, 57
Jones, Alexander, 164
Jung, Rex, 115
Jupiter, Great Red spot on, 39

K

Kijk, Corine, 72
Knoll, Andrew, 136
koalas, 141

L

language, 91
Lanza, Robert, 105
laughter, 73, 80–81
Leonardo da Vinci, 163
life, origin of, 136
light
    particle theory of, 10–11
    speed of, 19
lightning
    ball lightning, 129
    volcanic, 118
Lightspace, 66
limbic system, 84
limbs, artificial, 110–111
Lipo, Carl, 157
lithosphere, 120
loggerhead sea turtles, 138
longevity, 101
love, 96–97
low-energy nuclear reactions (LENRs), 16
Lu, Chensheng, 148
Lu, Ed, 48
Lyons, Leslie, 139

M

magnetic fields, sensing of, 137
magnetic poles, flipping of, 132
magnetoreception, 137
maladaptive brain plasticity, 111
male nipple, 109
Malhi, Yadvinder, 147
Malkin, Tamar, 111
mammoths, 144
mantle of Earth, 120
Marcus, Philip, 39
Marine Isotope Stage 19c, 127
Mars

bacteria on, 30
gravity on, 52
humans habitation of, 52–53
length of day on, 52
soil of, 52–53
temperature on, 52
water on, 30, 53
Martin, David, 100
massive astrophysical halo objects (MACHOs), 55
maximum temperature, 15
Mayan civilization, 165
McCarley, Robert, 78
McGinn, Colin, 99
megafauna, 146–147
megalodons, 146, 147
Melosh, Jay, 122
memory, 76–77
messenger pigeons, 137
meteorites, 122
migration of animals, 138
Milankovitch, Milutin, 127
Milankovitch cycles, 127
Milky Way galaxy, shape of, 49
Miller, Stanley, 136
mind uploading, 112
moai, 157
moon illusion, 32–33
moons, not orbited by other moons, 31
mountain ranges, 121
Mpemba, Erasto, 14
Mpemba effect, 14
Muller, Richard A., 127
multiverses, 50–51
Muñoz-Furlong, Anne, 75
muoncatalyzed fusion, 16
Musk, Elon, 53

N

National Ignition Facility (NIF), 20
Neanderthals, 158–159
near-death experiences (NDEs), 105
neonicotinoids, 148
neurons, in brain, 84, 87, 112
neurotransmitters, 76–77
neutrinos, 19
neutron stars, 29
Newton, Isaac, 10–11, 33, 60
Nickell, Joe, 22
nipple, male, 109

noise, made by cells, 82–83
nuclear fusion, 20–21
nuclear holocaust, 145

O

ocean, icicle formation on floor of, 133
omnidirectional treadmill, 66
Opportunity, rover, 30
optogenetics, 76–77
organs, replacement of, 110
Ornland, Kevin, 140
oxidative damage, 108
oxygen free radicals, 108
oxytocin, 96

P

Page, David, 90
Pagel, Mark, 95
parasites, 141
parietal lobe, of brain, 84, 85, 115
Parker, William, 103
Parnia, Sam, 105
particle theory of light, 10–11
Pavich, Milan, 119
Payne, Roger, 143
peanut allergies, 75
Pearce, Steven, 36
Pelling, Andrew, 82
Perlmutter, Saul, 42
pesticides, 148
Peters, Madelon, 72
phantom limb syndrome, 111
phenomenon colony collapse
  disorder (CCD), 148–149
photic sneeze reflex (PSR), 98
photoelectric effect, 10
piezoelectric effect, 128
pigeons, 137
pinky toe, 109
Piran, Tsvi, 57
Planck temperature, 15
planets, habitable, 40–41
plasticity of brain, 92
plate tectonics, 120–121
polycyclic aromatic hydrocarbons, 36
Pons, Stanley, 16
Ponzo illusion, 33
Portugal, Steven, 151

prefrontal cortex, 86
prosthetics, 110–111
protons, durability of, 18
Provine, Robert R., 73, 74, 81
Ptáček, Louis J., 98
pulsars, 29
Purcell, Chris, 49
pyramids, 166–167

Q

quantum physics, 99, 105

R

radiation exposure, 145
radioisotopes, 18
Raichle, Marcus, 87
Rapa Nui, 156
recombination, 90
relativity theory
  general, 35, 46, 60
  special, 19
rhinoceros, woolly, 147
RNA (ribonucleic acid), 106, 136
Roberts, Paul, 132
Roche, Edouard, 67
Rocky Mountain elk, migration of, 138
Roggeveen, Jacob, 156
Rosetta space probe, 131
Rossi, Andrea, 16
Rothenberg, David, 143

S

Sagittarius Dwarf galaxy, 49
Saladin, Kenneth, 109
Saturn, rings of, 67
Schinner, Andreas, 163
Schmidt, Brian, 42
sea turtles, migration of, 138
Search for Extraterrestrial
  Intelligence (SETI) Institute, 30, 31
senescence, 108
Sentinel telescope, 48
Shostak, Seth, 31
Simon, Theodore, 114
singing, by whales, 142–143
67P/Churyumov-Gerasimenko
  comet, 131
Skinner, Luke, 127

Skunkworks, 21
sleeping, 92–93
sneezing, from sunlight, 98
Snook, Richard, 83
space elevator, 58–59
SpaceX (company), 53
special theory of relativity, 19
Spergel, David N., 27
spontaneous human combustion
  (SHC), 22–23
stars, explosion of, 62–63. *See also*
  supernovas
Stonehenge, 154–155
subduction zones, 121
Sullivan, Andrew, 124
sunlight, sneezing from, 98
supernovas
  causes of, 62–63
  dark energy and, 42
  destruction of life on Earth by,
    68–69
synapses, 76–77
Szostak, Jack, 101

T

tailbone, 109
Taleyarkhan, Rusi, 16
Tan, Darren, 12
Taylor, Doris, 110
telomeres, 101, 108
temperature
  hottest, 15
  on Mars, 52
temporal lobe, of brain, 84
theory of general relativity, 35, 46,
  60
Thériault, Robert, 128
thermodynamics, 35
Thomas, Henry, 22
3D printing body parts, 110
Thurber, Andrew, 133
tickling, 73
time travel, 19
Toon, Brian, 122
tornadoes, fire, 124
Tuki, Suri, 157
Turner, Michael S., 42
Tutankhamen, 13

U

universe
  alternative universes, 50–51
  end of, 44–45
  expansion of, 44–45
  freezing of, 45
  shape of, 46–47

V

virtual reality, 66
virulent infectious diseases, 141
volcanic lightning, 118
vortices, 124
Voynich, Wilfrid, 162–163
Voynich Manuscript, 162–163

W

Wainwright, Geoff, 154
water
  as dinosaur urine, 123
  hot freezing faster than cold, 14
  on Mars, 30, 53
  origin of, 131
wave, whether light is, 10–11
wave-particle duality, 11
weakly interacting massive
  particles (WIMPS), 55
Weinberger, Norman, 85
whales, singing of, 142–143
wick effect, 22
Wilde, David, 105
Wood, Robert, 75

woolly mammoths, 144
woolly rhinoceros, 147
wormholes, 19

X

XNAs (xenonucleic acids), 106

Y

yawning, 74
Y chromosome, 90

Z

Zwicky, Fritz, 55